HISTORY HUNTING
IN THE YUKON

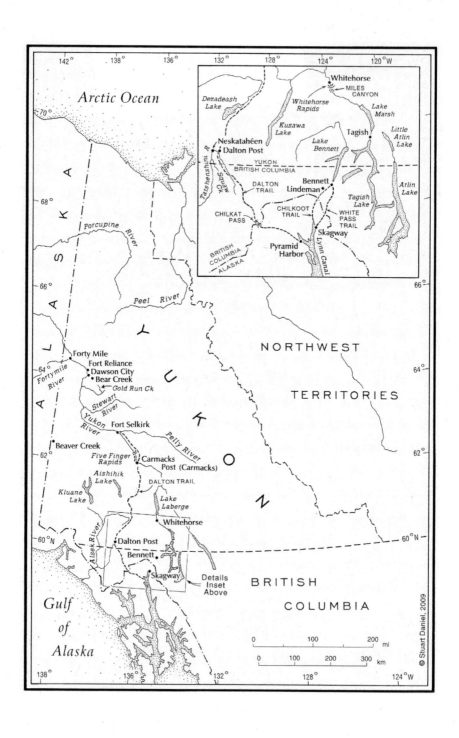

Arctic Ocean

ALASKA

YUKON

NORTHWEST

TERRITORIES

BRITISH

COLUMBIA

Gulf

of

Alaska

70°

68°

66°

64°

62°

60°N

66°

64°

62°

60°N

142°   138°   136°   132°   128°   124°   120°W

138°   136°   132°   128°   124°W

Porcupine   River

Peel   River

Forty Mile
Fort Reliance
Dawson City
Bear Creek
Gold Run Ck
Fortymile River
Stewart River
Yukon River
Fort Selkirk
Beaver Creek
Five Finger Rapids
Carmacks
Post (Carmacks)
Aishihik Lake
DALTON TRAIL
Kluane Lake
Lake Laberge
Whitehorse
Alsek River
Dalton Post
Bennett
Skagway
Details Inset Above
Pelly River

0   100   200 mi
0   100   200   300 km

© Stuart Daniel, 2009

Inset:

132°   128°   124°   120°W

Whitehorse
MILES CANYON
Dezadeash Lake
Whitehorse Rapids
Lake Marsh
Kusawa Lake
Neskatahéen
Dalton Post
Lake Bennett
Tagish
Little Atlin Lake
Tatshenshini R
Snaw Ck
YUKON
BRITISH COLUMBIA
DALTON TRAIL
Bennett
Lindeman
Atlin Lake
Tagish Lake
CHILKAT PASS
CHILKOOT TRAIL
WHITE PASS TRAIL
Skagway
BRITISH COLUMBIA
ALASKA
Pyramid Harbor
Lynn Canal

To Xenia and Tony
with best wishes from
the Yukon

HISTORY HUNTING
IN THE YUKON

Happy history hunting!

Michael Gates

Michael Gates
Whitehorse
Christmas 2016

**LOST
MOOSE**

First print on demand edition 2016

Lost Moose is an imprint of Harbour Publishing

Harbour Publishing Co. Ltd.
P.O. Box 219, Madeira Park, BC, V0N 2H0
www.harbourpublishing.com

Cover photograph (top) of northern lights near Lake Laberge by David Cartier.
Dawson City, 1898, courtesy Yukon Archives, Vancouver Public Library Fonds,
photo #02095
Edited by Carol Pope
Page 2 map by Stuart Daniel
Cover design by Anna Comfort
Printed and bound in Canada

Harbour Publishing acknowledges financial
support from the Government of Canada
through the Book Publishing Industry
Development Program and the Canada
Council for the Arts, and from the Province
of British Columbia through the BC Arts
Council and the Book Publishing Tax Credit.

Canada Council   Conseil des Arts
for the Arts   du Canada

BRITISH
COLUMBIA
ARTS COUNCIL
Supported by the Province of British Columbia

Library and Archives Canada Cataloguing in Publication

Gates, Michael, 1949–
    History hunting in the Yukon / Michael Gates.

ISBN 978-1-55017-477-9

1. Yukon–History. I. Title.

FC4011.G38 2010   971.9'1   C2010-900046-3

For my wife Kathy who, more than anyone else,
has made this book possible.

Contents

Acknowledgements   9
How I Became a History Hunter   11

FIRST NATIONS
Tatshenshini Expedition Yields More Adventure than History   17
Wilderness is Actually an Area Rich in Human History   22
There's a Dramatic Story behind the Kohklux Map   26
Jim Boss Started the Land-Claim Process   31
Vanished First Nation Architecture Reveals Rich History   35
Little John Site Yields Evidence of First Canadians   39
Dam History Forecasts Catastrophe on the Alsek   44
Ice and Snow Yield Secrets of the Past   48

THE EARLY DAYS
The Fortymile River Makes for Challenging History   55
The Force in the North: the First Mounties   60
The Mounted Police in Forty Mile   64
Showdown on Glacier Creek   69
Frederick Schwatka's Forgotten Expedition   74
Tom Williams' Golden Death March   78

THE KLONDIKE GOLD RUSH
Death on the Chilkoot Trail   85
Tagish Post was a Major Klondike Stop   90
The House that Gold Built   94
How the Mounties Got Their Man   99
Early Gold Mining in the Yukon was a Steamy Affair   104
Smells Like Gold Rush Spirit   109

THE DALTON TRAIL

Jack Dalton and the Shooting of Dan McGinnis   115
Escape from Famine   120
One Woman's Gold Rush   124
The Hellish Reindeer Caper of 1898   130
Cattle Drives to the Yukon   134
Dead Horses on the Dalton Trail   138

LEGENDARY PEOPLE

The Real-Life Legend of Klondike Joe Boyle   145
Robert Service's Secret Love Life   149
The Pioneer Woman of Squaw Creek   154
Martha Black was a Woman of the North   158
Early Gold Recorders Kept Order on the Creeks   162
Bill Gates: Klondike Casanova or Gold-Rush Gouger?   166
Is Father Judge a Forgotten Hero?   170
The Case of the Drunken Diplomat   175
A Canadian Poser Governed Alaska for Five Years   180

EXTRAORDINARY EVENTS

The Colourful World of Early Yukon Politics   187
High Times Continue in the Yukon   192
It was the "Wets" vs. the "Drys" in the Battle of the Booze   197
Christmas a Special Celebration in the Yukon   201
The Little School that Saved the Yukon   205
Terrorism in the Klondike   209
"Languorous Lilies of Soulless Love"   213

HISTORY, HISTORY EVERYWHERE

History Revealed in Old Tin Cans   221
There's Film in Them Thar Hills   225
The Cabin on Gold Run Claim Number 24   230
Fond Memories of Life at Bear Creek   234
The Secret Language of Gold   239
Coming of Age in the Goldfields   244
The Yukon River Breakup Brings a Flood of Excitement   249

Index   254

Acknowledgements

I would like to express my thanks to a small number of individuals. This list could be much longer, but I know that if I attempted to name all the wonderful people who have contributed to this work, I would be sure to miss someone. May I simply say that I deeply appreciate the numerous exchanges I have had with the many generous and articulate individuals who have shared their stories and expertise with me.

There are, however, a few people I must name. First and foremost, there is my wife, Kathy, who has helped me in so many ways. Consistently, she tolerates my incessant chatter about one historical topic after another. I have bounced countless ideas off her, and she has provided me with steady support and constructive feedback on my writing.

I appreciate the fact that Richard Mostyn, editor of the *Yukon News*, thought my idea of a *History Hunter* column was a good one, and that Erling Friis-Bastaad, who edits most of my copy, has improved the quality of my work.

I would also like to acknowledge the editorial persistence of Carol Pope, who ground off the coarse burrs and put a polish to this volume.

There are people at various institutions with whom I have interacted over the years: The Yukon Archives staff has been especially accommodating. The archives are a rich repository of vital historical documents, and there are so many there who have helped me, I fear I will unintentionally forget someone if I attempt to name them all.

The group at the EMR library, in the Elijah Smith Building in Whitehorse, have continually been helpful and encouraging.

The staff at Parks Canada in Dawson City, most notably my colleagues Paula Hassard, Louise Ranger and Leslie Piercy, and David Neufeld in Whitehorse, have always been supportive of my efforts.

A number of individuals in the Tourism and Culture department of the Yukon Government have been generous in assisting my efforts since I started on this amazing historical journey. You have all helped to make my work with history fulfilling.

In Alaska, Judy Munns, director of the Skagway Museum, Karl Gurcke of the US National Park Service, and the people at the Alaska State Historical Library in Juneau all gave me assistance when I needed it.

To all of these institutions and people, plus many more, I owe my gratitude. These are the heroes who collectively are keeping our history alive.

How I Became a History Hunter

What exactly is a History Hunter?

There is no formal definition; simply a passion for understanding days gone by. The History Hunter is consumed by a desire to unravel the truth about time past with an almost manic passion. The History Hunter is driven with a steely determination to seek out the story of every landscape, hear the narrative of each person, rummage through the pages of every archive, and look for evidence of life long ago in every artifact.

My wife, Kathy, says I'm like a kid in a candy shop when it comes to history. That's true: I've been looking through the history window of the Yukon candy store for nearly four decades now—and I still haven't lost my appetite.

I started my university studies dreaming of becoming an archeologist and carving my way through the rainforest to explore the ancient ruins of Central America. I never got there because the Yukon happened instead.

In 1971, I had taken a year off to earn money to pay for another year of study. With two jobs I was making plenty, nevertheless driving the bungs into beer kegs on a brewery conveyor belt and operating a shrink-wrap machine didn't appeal to this young lad in his early twenties.

Luckily for me, I received a call from Jim Bennett, a graduate student in archeology at the University of Calgary who was looking for an assistant. "Would you like to go to the Yukon?" he asked. "When do you want to leave?" I replied. A couple of days later, we hit the road for the great north in a 1949 Mercury one-ton truck full of gear and loaded down with eager aspirations. When our vehicle gave up outside Fort Nelson, we did not, and somehow we managed to make it to Kluane Lake where my forty-year adventure began.

I learned from my first two summers of exploration that the Yukon is loaded with incredible stories of lives lived and places that are no more. But even more apparent to me was that this history is fragile and that if someone didn't grasp onto it, it would slip away. So I put aside my fanciful notions of becoming an archeologist slashing through the Yucatan jungles in search of ancient temples, and instead turned my sights northward where I have dedicated my life to seeking the historical treasures of the Yukon.

I started collecting old animal bones as a child, and with them opened my first museum in our basement at ten years old, charging neighbourhood kids five cents for a look. At university, I studied archeology and worked in the field for five seasons. I catalogued artifacts at the Glenbow Museum, recorded buildings for the Canadian Inventory of Historic Building, practised museum-artifact conservation at the Canadian Conservation Institute, and worked on land-use planning in the Yukon. All these disciplines and experiences—and more—became integral in my work at Parks Canada in Dawson City and eventually Whitehorse for over thirty years. I provided consultation on cultural resources, and organized, preserved, studied and developed displays—using one of the finest collections of artifacts in northern Canada.

Over the years, I have wandered over hills and into valleys, following the trails left on the landscape by travellers of old. What I've learned in the process is that the human imprint in the Yukon is scattered everywhere—frozen in the ice and snow, sitting on mountaintops and buried beneath buildings. From the humblest tin can to a four-thousand-ton mining behemoth, I have learned to respect and appreciate every inkling of the past. History anywhere is a rich treasure, and nowhere is it more fascinating than in the Yukon. Stories of survival and human spirit are bigger than life in this frozen place.

Even today in the Yukon, at minus fifty degrees Celsius, the obstacles are immense. Batteries don't produce current. Oil turns to fudge and rubber becomes peanut brittle. Planes don't fly and buses don't drive. At our extreme temperatures, making a trip from Dawson City to Vancouver or Edmonton can be like flying to the moon. In the Yukon, all those inaccessible points on the planet will perpetually be the "Outside." And inside this frozen place, we are linked to the land and each other by the language of gold, by the timeless agents of nature, by lusty legends of violence and valour, and by a human history of innovation against incredible odds.

And that is why I am a History Hunter.

FIRST NATIONS

Tatshenshini Expedition Yields More Adventure than History

One of my first efforts at history hunting was a failure. Fired with determination to find a historic site on the Tatshenshini River, I engaged an outfitter in 1972 to take us there. We reached the location I thought we were looking for but had to turn back without finding the physical remains we sought. Along the way, though, we experienced many thrills courtesy of Mother Nature, and I realized that history hunting is as much about the journey as what you seek . . .

The grizzly came up along our right flank, but it wasn't until he crossed into the valley and started to follow us that I became uneasy. These lowlands were flat and barren, almost a kilometre across with forty-metre cliffs along each side. There was nowhere to go but downstream toward the Tatshenshini River. The trek on this dull overcast day had been long and exhausting, and our group was strung out almost a kilometre along our route. The appearance of the grizzly injected a surge of energy into our efforts to find a camp for the night. It wasn't the first grizzly bear we saw on that trip, nor the last—just the most memorable.

At that point, it was hard to remember my original objective. This was to locate the remains of the old village of *Noogaayík* on the bank of the Tatshenshini River. The quest had been initiated the year before when I was assisting University of Calgary archeology graduate student Jim Bennett in a project in the southwest Yukon.

One day we were at the village of Champagne talking to elder Johnny Fraser. He was bent with age but had bright, alert eyes as he talked about the old village on the Tatshenshini River. Many of the First Nation families in the southwest Yukon have roots leading back to this village and to a period when there was regular commerce along the "Tat." Originally called the Alsek by the Native people of the area, the river later became known as the Tatshenshini. Through time, the traditional trade and family connections with the coast via this river have been lost. The region is now popularly characterized as a pristine wilderness.

The first white men to travel through this area may have been Edward J. Glave, an Englishman and renowned African explorer, and his companion Jack Dalton, well-known frontiersman and Alaskan pioneer. They departed on foot from Neskatahéen (the First Nation community near which Dalton Post was later established) in August 1890 and hiked down the valley toward the coast until they came to "the Alseck fishing camp" where there were two hundred people all engaged in fishing from the abundant salmon run. There the gaunt adventurers were greeted with great hospitality and provided with food and a tent for the duration of their stay. Next, they continued downriver in a dugout canoe with Shank, the Chilkat "medicine man," as their guide, until they reached the Alaskan coast.

From Glave's description of the Alsek/Tatshenshini there was abundant evidence of human occupation along the shores of the great wilderness river. This account, combined with Johnny Fraser's references, were what had stirred Jim Bennett to visit the vicinity in 1972.

A year later Bennett had dropped out of graduate school and by default I inherited his project. This is how I found myself departing Neskatahéen in southwest Yukon for the Tatshenshini River. The party included my guide Art Brewster, his young son Dale, his wrangler Tom Wild, graduate-student Frances Roback, and a team of pack horses to carry the supplies.

The weather was warm and sunny so we made good time camping the first night near an abandoned cabin. The following morning I found a case of sweating dynamite behind our sleeping quarters. Dynamite in this condition is highly unstable and can explode unexpectedly. Perhaps this was an omen

E.J. Glave, the English explorer, found the Tatshenshini River valley to be filled with evidence of early inhabitants. *FRANK LESLIE'S ILLUSTRATED NEWSPAPER*, 1890–1891

to suggest danger would accompany us on this journey. When I returned to Haines Junction I reported the explosives to the RCMP.

That day we had ascended a series of steep switchbacks. Larry, one of the pack horses, fell off the edge and landed on the switchback below, shaken but unharmed. After repacking, we started off again. Later, Art had to stop to adjust the panniers once more. He reflected it was the most difficult day he had ever had with his horses.

The following day we headed across country with no trail to follow. At one point we observed two magnificent bull moose with heads down and antlers locked in combat. The experience of this magnificent wildlife was an unexpected bonus. We had frequent sightings of moose, bear, sheep, goats and various small game throughout the trip.

This area had not seen many people in recent times and had become densely overgrown with willow, which slowed our procession to a crawl. Art and Tom had to battle the dense undergrowth with axes. At one stop, I dismounted my horse, Chief, and went forward to investigate. The branches were so thickly intertwined that I was walking a metre and a half above solid ground, and then suddenly I found myself on a web of branches with thirty metres of air below me. I carefully retraced my steps to the edge of the embankment! We eventually were able to descend a steep talus slope onto the barren glacial outwash valley where we were stalked by the grizzly.

It was another day of slow progress before we reached the Tatshenshini River. Humans and animals alike were exhausted and hungry. With our gear unceremoniously piled on a sandbar we assessed our situation. Behind us flowed the Tatshenshini River, dark and fast. The area was densely overgrown. The chances of identifying exposures that would reveal archeological remains seemed remote. Worse yet, there was nothing for the pack horses to eat. Art was concerned for their well-being and recommended a retreat to more nutritious terrain.

On our return we had another two days of difficult travel before we regained the trail that we had used for the first part of our journey. During that time another horse collapsed and fell twenty-five metres down a steep slope we were ascending. This time it was a mare that during our travels had been feeding a foal as well as packing supplies. Fortunately she was uninjured. We transferred her load to the panniers on the other pack horses and carried on. On this portion of our expedition we found signs of human life. We camped in a small grassy meadow one evening where we found evidence of an old campsite and fragments of a small white rubber boot. I wondered who else had been to such a remote place, but never found an answer.

We travelled through cool, wet and windy weather for the final three days. When we finally arrived back at Neskatahéen we were all thankful to have made it in one piece. And the grizzly that circled us? We never saw him again.

In the end the journey yielded little of historical nature but plenty of adventure. We had travelled for nine days through some of the wildest country in the Yukon. If the quest is as important as finding the object of your search then this adventure was laden with treasure.

Each time I drive the Haines Road past the turnoff to Dalton Post, I stop at the roadside viewpoint and look off to the southwest. In the distance I can see the cleft in the mountains through which the Tatshenshini flows. I still feel a pull from the place we tried to find so many years ago. Perhaps I will be able to return some day.

As long as there is one quest left, one unfulfilled goal to achieve, one place to which you wish to return, then life is definitely worth living.

Wilderness is Actually an Area Rich in Human History

As you learn more about the history of a place, your perception of it and of the world changes. Two years after writing about my Tatshenshini adventure, I reflected on what lessons I had learned from the experience. We frequently try to shape the world to fit our preconceived notions of it, often like trying to fit an oversized foot into a tight but fashionable shoe. This, to some extent, was how I viewed the "wilderness-adventure" industry, which promotes the image of "pristine" wilderness where humans have never before travelled. I long ago learned that a good fit makes more sense than fashion . . .

"Wilderness: wĭ'lderness n. uncultivated and uninhabited land or tract."

— Oxford Illustrated Dictionary

"The most intact, undisturbed wild natural areas left on our planet—those last truly wild places that humans do not control and have not developed with roads, pipelines or other industrial infrastructure."

—What is a Wilderness Area, *The WILD Foundation, www.wild.org/main/about/what-is-a-wilderness-area*

"Even today the Tatshenshini offers an uncommon pristine wilderness experience, free for the most part from the evidence of man and his works."

—*www.wildernessadventures.ca/TatshenshiniRiverRaft.html*

Modern society has constructed the concept of wilderness as places of untainted nature, devoid of humans, where animal species can propagate without fear of extinction due to urban sprawl, overhunting or pollution. "Pristine" is the overworked term used to describe these areas. But it's a lie and I will tell you why this is so.

When European immigrants came to North America centuries ago, they perceived a land populated only by small numbers of "savages." This notion of an unpopulated new world was later accepted by people of the twentieth century, prompting a countermovement against urban development and the despoiling of nature, a determination to preserve the remaining areas yet relatively undamaged by human impact. While I applaud the efforts that have championed the setting aside of "wilderness" from urban and industrial encroachment, I caution my readers to think about these places also as human landscapes. Charles C. Mann wrote an excellent book a few years ago, titled *1491*, in which he demonstrated effectively that the so-called New World was more densely populated before Europeans arrived than we have come to believe. He illustrates that there were well-developed civilizations in North and South America before the Egyptian dynasties. In some cases, he argues, as disease decimated the aboriginal populations, ecosystems responded by changing dramatically. Cultivated fields gave way to forests, and populations of certain species, like passenger pigeons, exploded. In essence, humans were once a keystone species in these environments. So what happened? It's a complicated story, but one of the critical elements that must be understood is the role disease had in decimating indigenous populations. The original inhabitants had no natural resistance to the diseases introduced by Europeans. Perhaps 90 percent of the resident populations died as they succumbed to one illness after another, resulting in massive social disintegration that made it much easier for Europeans to move in. What the early settlers encountered was not wilderness but huge tracts of land recently depopulated by preceding waves of smallpox, diphtheria and tuberculosis. Take the Tatshenshini.

In 1972, I made a nine-day trip down the Tatshenshini River and did not see a single human outside of my travelling party. We encountered dense bush, a wide array of wildlife and endless awe-inspiring natural beauty. Yet even in the most isolated reaches of our journey, we found evidence that people had been there before us. The Tatshenshini, now touted as one of the world's premiere wilderness-rafting rivers, was once a transportation corridor filled with people. The discovery of Kwädạy Dän Ts'ìnchị, the famous mummy found frozen in ice in the Tatshenshini-Alsek Park, is only the most prominent evidence of this fact. This young man was making his way in to the Tatshenshini River two hundred years ago when he perished. Whether he was travelling alone or in a group is not clear, nor is the manner of his death. What we do understand is that he was following a well-known trail to a river that served as an important avenue for living, moving and trading. E.J. Glave, noted English explorer and the first European to document the region, reported in 1890 abundant evidence of people living on the Tatshenshini.

Venturing downriver from the Southern Tutchone village of Neskatahéen, Glave and Jack Dalton encountered a settlement that stretched for two and one-half kilometres along the river, with discrete fishing camps every 300 metres or so along the bank. Shielded from the wind by brush piles, each consisted of small tent shelters or one or two small log huts roofed with hemlock bark. Goods were stored in above-ground caches, and large quantities of salmon that had been gaffed in the river were hanging to dry.

Glave recounted how people from the coast, known as the Nuqua, came upriver, settled on the Tat and established trade with the Gunena (Southern Tutchone) from the interior. By the time Glave visited the river, the settlements had dwindled away, leaving decaying buildings and only a few descendants who had intermarried with the interior people as evidence.

Many of the inhabitants had died from European diseases like smallpox and influenza; others had been washed away in the mid-1800s when a dam of ice farther up the Alsek River gave way, unleashing a giant wall of water that scoured out everything in its path. Some of the Yukon elders born before the turn of the twentieth century grew up in this area, living on the Tatshenshini and travelling the river between the coast and the interior. Their stories were documented by the late Catharine McClellan, the highly respected anthropologist from the University of Wisconsin who worked in the Yukon from 1949 until she retired from teaching.

Only the most preliminary archeological reconnaissance has been undertaken in this area, which is isolated and difficult to get to, so the potential for discovering further evidence of human occupation still lies before us. I have no doubt it is there, waiting to be revealed with the passage of time.

What we have to do is adjust our thinking around the concept of wilderness. We cannot continue to look at areas like the Tatshenshini as wilderness devoid of human associations. People have blanketed the landscape of the southwest Yukon for at least ten thousand years. It is only in recent times, due to changing circumstances, that the Tatshenshini was vacated.

We must regard people as an integral part of the ecology, perhaps playing a critical role in the formation of the complex web of interrelations, and we should celebrate that fact.

Whenever I look west toward the brilliant white-peaked range of mountains visible from the Haines Road, the view calls to me. In this broad vista, I see a natural landscape, but one with the human imprint upon it.

After all, we can't really pretend that no one ever lived there.

There's a Dramatic Story behind the Kohklux Map

The Kohklux map is one of the most remarkable documents of Yukon history from before the gold rush. It was created by a Chilkat Tlingit chief from Klukwan, Alaska. He had never worked with pencil and paper before, which makes his map even more remarkable...

Robert Campbell knew there was going to be trouble from the moment the twenty-seven Chilkats arrived in several boats at Fort Selkirk. There was only a handful of staff at the Hudson's Bay trading post that day on August 20, 1852.

The Hudson's Bay Company trading post was strategically located on the mighty Yukon River where the Pelly River joins it from the east. A half a century later, the Canadian government briefly considered making Fort Selkirk the capital of the Yukon, but at this moment in this isolated spot, the very lives of the European occupants of the settlement were at risk.

The Chilkats outnumbered and outgunned Campbell's party and he knew from the outset that they were in danger. Campbell soon found himself staring down the barrel of a loaded musket and barely avoiding being stabbed as he struggled against the intruders. There was little the company traders could do but stand by helplessly as the post was pillaged and their lives threatened.

Detail of the Kohklux Map. CHIEF KOHKLUX, GEORGE DAVIDSON, "MAP SHOWING
ROUTE FROM CHILKAT RIVER, NORTHERN BRITISH COLUMBIA, TO FORT SELKIRK, YUKON
TERRITORY," 1852 (1883), LIBRARY AND ARCHIVES CANADA, H3/703/1852(1883), NMC 36636

Campbell deployed his staff in several key buildings that evening in the
hope of protecting their supplies, but marauders wandered the site all night
boldly getting into mischief. The Europeans didn't get much sleep, and the
following day things got worse.

On August 22, Campbell and his party fled the post by canoe and put
ashore a few kilometres downstream. At some point during the excitement of
the Chilkat raid, Mrs. Flett, wife of one of his staff, gave birth to a baby boy.

The following day, Campbell and his party returned on foot to the now-
abandoned trading post. Any supplies not taken away were strewn about,
destroyed. The buildings were vandalized and the post rendered unliveable.

Fully expecting the company to support him in the re-provision of the post, Campbell left shortly after the raid, making his way back over the Hudson's Bay Company trade route to the headquarters thousands of kilometres away—but his request was denied. The great trading company did not return to Fort Selkirk until well into the twentieth century. Thirty years after the raid all that remained of the post were the crumbling ruins of the stone fireplaces.

The Chilkat raid was nothing more than a move by the coastal people to protect their monopoly on trade with the people of the interior. Long before the white man arrived in the Pacific Northwest, the Tlingit people of the coast had a well-developed commerce with the people of the Yukon. They gained access to these markets through various coastal routes such as the Chilkoot and Chilkat Passes on the Lynn Canal. The Chilkat people of Lynn Canal controlled these accesses and aggressively maintained control of trade and movement into the interior till as late as 1890.

The Hudson's Bay Company trading post at Fort Selkirk therefore posed a challenge to Chilkat trade that could not be ignored. Thus, in 1852, the party from Klukwan, a Chilkat Tlingit village near modern-day Haines, looted and destroyed the post and ensured their continued dominance of trade in the region for another forty years.

Thirty years after the destruction of Fort Selkirk, the stone chimneys were all that remained. *A SUMMER IN ALASKA*, FREDERICK SCHWATKA, 1883

They entered the Yukon via the Chilkat Pass and Kusawa Lake, from which they travelled downriver by boat until they reached the Yukon River and eventually Fort Selkirk. Returning to the coast after the raid, the party travelled up the Yukon River as far as present-day Carmacks, then overland to the Chilkat Pass and back to Klukwan.

Nearly twenty years later, Dr. George Davidson, the noted geographer who in 1867 had surveyed the region, returned to Alaska to view the eclipse of the sun slated to occur August 7, 1869. Kohklux, leader of the Chilkats at Klukwan, was approached by Davidson for permission to view the event from their village. Kohklux had accompanied his father, who led the raid on Fort Selkirk in 1852.

Kohklux was a man, according to Davidson, of "commanding presence, nearly six feet high, broad chest and well-formed head . . ." who "carried a bullet-hole in his cheek" and was renowned as a great warrior and diplomat. Through Kohklux, Davidson's passage to Klukwan and the viewing of the eclipse transpired without incident. After the event, Davidson drew the leader a diagram that described how the eclipse had occurred.

In exchange, Kohklux told the story of how he had participated in the destruction of Fort Selkirk seventeen years before. Assisted by his two wives, over the course of two or three days, they sketched a map of the route followed to and from Fort Selkirk. This was the first time that Kohklux and his wives had used pencil and paper. According to Davidson, who wrote down on their map his best phonetic rendering of the Chilkat place names, Kohklux and his wives were mystified by the scientist's ability to repeat the names they had given him. Built from memories of the trip taken years before, the map showed lakes, streams, rapids and mountains. Distances were charted not by degrees of latitude and longitude, but by days of travel.

The map Davidson eventually published in 1901 was not the original Kohklux rendering but a more traditional cartographer's version that included many place names provided by Kohklux, as well as by European recorders. The Kohklux original vanished into the mists of time.

That is, until 1984, when Linda Johnson, then an archivist with the Yukon Archives, earned the honourable title of "History Hunter" when on a holiday trip to California she identified the original Kohklux map as part of a new acquisition at the Bancroft Library. A few years later, the Bancroft

Library agreed to loan the original map for display at a Yukon Historical and Museums Association conference held in Whitehorse.

In 1995, I participated in a gathering at Fort Selkirk where members of the current-day Chilkat Tlingit joined those of the Selkirk First Nation and other Yukon residents in an encounter much friendlier than that of 143 years earlier.

The Kohklux map is one of the most important documents pertaining to the Yukon dating from the nineteenth century. First Nations people have a long and intimate relationship with the landscape of the Yukon, their homeland—gained through first-hand encounters over a lifetime, and the accumulated familiarity of many generations. Because this intelligence has traditionally been passed down by word of mouth, it was a rare and significant event that Kohklux and his wives chose to capture their knowledge graphically through a medium they were unaccustomed to using.

What's in a map? There is more to a map than the mere physical portrayal of a place. A map is a cultural artifact—and the full meaning of the Kohklux map as a social document is yet to be known.

Jim Boss Started the Land-Claim Process

In future, our descendants will look back on the establishment of land claims as one of the defining events in the Yukon during the twentieth century. Through land claims, the First Nations of the Yukon have been given back parcels of land important to their communities and regained some control of their own affairs through self-government. Land claims have given recognition to the fact that Europeans usurped First Nations land, and denied the people a voice. Jim Boss was the first to champion a land claim and the right of his people to control their own destiny.

In early 1902 Chief Jim Boss (Kashxóot) of the Southern Tutchone people living around Lake Laberge approached Whitehorse lawyer T.W. Jackson to write a letter to the government. He wanted to request compensation for the loss of lands and hunting grounds by the incursion of the white man during the recent gold rush.

He had previously requested that William Ogilvie, commissioner of the Yukon, set aside 1,600 acres of land on the upper end of Lake Laberge for his people. Ogilvie acknowledged the long-term occupation of the site by aboriginal people, and on July 13, 1900, the Canadian government set aside a reserve, reduced to 320 acres, "... for the use of the Indians in the vicinity."

Boss may not have been impressed with the reduced allocation granted by

Jim Boss was the first to advance a Yukon land claim to the government of Canada. YUKON ARCHIVES, BLACKWELL COLLECTION, 91/38 PHO 417-2

the commissioner, so the letter, written January 13, 1902, was directed instead to the superintendent of Indian Affairs in Ottawa. ". . . before the advent of the white man," wrote Jackson, "the Indians had no difficulty in procuring game sufficient to their wants whereas at the present time, because of the white trappers and hunters taking possession of the country the Indians are unable to subsist as they were formally able to do." If the government was willing to entertain the proposal, Boss offered to gather the people of the region together at any time.

This is the first-known attempt of the First Nation people of the Yukon to enter into land-claim negotiations with the government of Canada. The government ignored the request, and so began a process that was to continue for nearly a century before reaching its conclusion. For some First Nations, it is still not yet complete.

Similarly, in 1933, Joe Squam of the Teslin people claimed land in the Wolf Lake area, stating that he had ". . . hunted and trapped over this land since a child." The government hastily denied his claim too.

The formal process that has resulted in eleven Final Agreements in the Yukon Territory started in 1973 when a proposal for the settlement of land claims entitled "Together Today for our Children Tomorrow" was submitted to Prime Minister Pierre Trudeau. It had been a long time coming.

Boss was born about 1871. His father, Mundessa, originally from the Hutchi area, fifty kilometres north of the village of Champagne, was chief of the people living around Lake Laberge. His mother, Lande, was from Tagish southeast of Whitehorse. Many of the Taʼan Kwächʼän of today can trace their ancestry back to this couple and their descendants.

Boss lived in the Whitehorse area until his death in 1950 and during his life had three wives. He first married Kathleen Kitty and adopted her son Fred. His second wife was Maude, with whom he had four children: Alice, David, Lena and Ned. Maude died in the influenza epidemic of 1918. With his third wife, Annie, he had two more offspring, Agnes and Sam.

Considered by his people to be a successful and wealthy man, Boss adapted well to the economic opportunities made possible by the influx of newcomers that resulted from the gold rush. He supplied firewood and fish to the sternwheelers that plied the waters of the Yukon, and provided wild meat to the Burns meat outlet in Whitehorse. Despite the messy nature of this work, he was well known for keeping an extremely tidy camp.

Boss built a roadhouse on Lake Laberge and subsequently operated several others during his life, in addition to a fox farm during the period of high prices. He owned several houses and a team of horses to transport him back and forth. He held several potlatches over the years, including one across the river from Whitehorse in 1905 that lasted several days. In his later years, he was frequently seen attending events in Whitehorse decked out in specially made regalia, some of which is now housed in the MacBride Museum of Yukon History.

Because of his family connections, linguistic skills and ability to adapt to and successfully exploit the new economy, Boss was widely respected within his own society, and also acknowledged by the white community. On more than one occasion, he represented his people's interests to the government and acted as a go-between. Had the government entertained the negotiation of a treaty, Boss would have been the obvious choice to bring people together for such a purpose. Unfortunately, this was not to be, and it was left to another leader, Elijah Smith, to advance the First Nations cause to Prime Minister Trudeau many years later.

In December of 2000, the Historic Sites and Monuments Board of Canada recommended to the Minister of the Environment that Chief Jim Boss (Kashxóot) be recognized as a person of national significance "because he provided guidance and inspiration to the Yukon First Nations in their struggle for survival through the important transition from traditional lifestyle to the introduction of European social, economic and political systems at the turn of the twentieth century."

On January 13, 2002, precisely one hundred years after his letter was submitted to the government suggesting that a treaty be negotiated, representatives from the Ta'an Kwäch'än Council, the government of Canada, and the government of Yukon formally signed the Ta'an Kwäch'än Council Final Agreement in a public ceremony. The Final Agreement included provisions covering financial compensation, transfer of 785 square kilometres of land to the Ta'an Kwäch'än Council, protection of heritage values, opportunities for economic development and creation of a new level of self-government for the First Nation.

Featured on the cover of the Ta'an Kwäch'än Council Final Agreement is an image of Chief Jim Boss dressed in ceremonial regalia. I wonder if he would have been pleased with the outcome of this momentous agreement, given the nature of the complaints he voiced a century before. I think the answer would be yes.

Vanished First Nation Architecture Reveals Rich History

*As a student, I fell under the thrall of the Yukon. Continually wanting
to return, I fabricated a reason for doing so, which was to record the
location of historical log buildings. I also took my fishing rod to provide
both diversion and nutrition during my travels, especially when I went
off-road. In the course of undertaking these recording trips, I developed
a deep interest in all of the vernacular architecture in the Yukon . . .*

It was a hot, dry, sunny day in 1977 when I returned to find the plundered
remains. At the edge of a grassy clearing along the bank of Village Creek
in the southwest Yukon, hewn log planks were randomly scattered in the
brush and protruding from the creek bank. This confirmed my worst fears
that some of the Yukon's finest First Nation architecture had been destroyed
by human action.

On previous visits here, my attention had focussed on the standing remains of the old site of the village of Neskatahéen on the Tatshenshini River,
two kilometres or so from Dalton Post. In 1972 another student and I had
made a simple sketch map of some of the key features at the site.

I had learned of the damage to the site earlier from various individuals,
including my mentor, Alan Innes-Taylor. The bulldozed remains of several
log cabins were still evident in the nearby site of Dalton Post, which seemed

to support the stories that in the 1960s, a small exploration company looking for copper exposures in the nearby mountains had recklessly flattened some of the historic buildings to make way for a camp or parking lot.

The timbers now buried along the edge of Village Creek that skirted Neskatahéen were carefully flattened planks that had been shaped with hand tools and broad axes or adzes, from locally procured timber. They exemplified perhaps the most articulate examples of aboriginal construction in the Yukon. It would have taken tremendous effort for the builders to gather the wood, shape and split the large timbers and erect the structures. These ruins reveal much about the community and the trade system that supported it.

There are some intriguing archival photographs taken at the turn of the twentieth century by gold-rush stampeders and government geologists that reveal the fine construction of a dozen or so log buildings at Neskatahéen in the style of the longhouses of the Chilkat people of the Alaskan coast. They were large rectangular structures, and the best of them had a front perspective made from carefully squared horizontally placed eight metre-long planks slotted into four metre-long upright timbers positioned at each corner and extending a metre or so above the roofline. The side walls were similarly assembled, but allowed for greater length. Some of the buildings had additional upright posts midway from front to back to allow for another row of planks to be installed.

The pitch of the roof was shallow, creating a massive front façade. Positioned in the centre of the roof peak was a large smoke hole, around which a skeletal wooden frame was constructed.

The only opening for most of the buildings was a wooden door, accessible from a raised platform on the front façade. One photo, though, reveals a building with several windows. Another photograph shows a building of similar design, with the familiar plank façade, roofline and smoke hole, but the side walls appear to be made of logs left in the round.

One illustration of an interior reveals what appears to be a wooden platform or floor constructed around a large firepit. I conjure up images of the dim, smoky interior with an open blaze situated in the centre of the space and smoke gently rising through the opening in the roof. Members of one or more families would have enjoyed the warmth of the flames.

At Klukwan, Alaska, and other First Nation communities along the

This splendid hewn-log structure located at Neskatahéen in 1898 displays the influence of the Tlingit style of longhouse construction.
MACBRIDE MUSEUM OF YUKON HISTORY, ACC #1898-30-106

coast, the construction of such houses reached a high art, which is mirrored more simply by the examples at Neskatahéen. In the large old coastal structures, several related families lived together, each having its own defined area within. I wonder whether the smaller Yukon versions were utilized in a similar fashion.

The buildings at Neskatahéen represent the extension of Chilkat Tlingit influence into the Yukon. Neskatahéen was an important trade centre not only for the coastal people along the Lynn Canal, but also for those of the lower Tatshenshini and Dry Bay areas. Neskatahéen was a bicultural and bilingual community, where extensive intermarriage between the Tlingit of the coast and the Southern Tutchone people of the interior cemented trade links between specific families. There was an active exchange of goods between the two groups. From the interior, various raw and finished furs, lichen (used as a dye), goat wool, copper, and perhaps even obsidian were traded for eulachon fish and oil, cedar boxes and decorative dentalia shells.

Later, the Chilkat added a variety of European items to their inventory of trade goods. This trade network continued until Jack Dalton broke the monopoly over the Chilkat Pass in the 1890s, and then was largely finished off by the events surrounding the Klondike gold rush.

Because of the abundant supply of salmon in the Village and Klukshu creeks, hundreds of people including those from as far away as Hutchi and Aishihik would assemble to exploit the annual salmon runs. Even today, this area is an important source of food for the people who live in the region. In 2004, I had the privilege of participating in a summer camp for First Nation youth where the technique of gaffing salmon was demonstrated to and practised by the excited crowd of young people.

By 1890, Neskatahéen had probably reached its zenith as an important population and trade centre. The extended network of communities down the Tatshenshini River had faded, and the twentieth century had yet to leave its mark.

Later, the new trading post established nearby by Jack Dalton diminished the original community. As well, restrictions imposed by the Canadian government over the years to ensure sovereignty, followed by the establishment of Kluane Game Sanctuary, limited access to resources. Further erosion of its importance occurred when the Alaska Highway was built and communities gravitated to that newly created corridor.

By the 1970s no one lived at Neskatahéen anymore. Deserted and unprotected, it was exposed to the elements and vulnerable to human intrusion. The magnificent old longhouses had disappeared, survived only by a couple of structures built in the twentieth century, whose declining shells still stand today. The place, now known by the Southern Tutchone form of Shäwshe (which sounds something like Shaw-shay), is recognized by land claims and lies in a protected area along the newly designated Tatshenshini heritage river. While the Tat continues to erode the bank closer and closer to the old village, its memory and the wonderful buildings that once stood there will not be forgotten.

Little John Site Yields Evidence of First Canadians

When archeologist Norm Easton described the archeological context of the Little John site to me, I could imagine the people and animals moving across the landscape thousands of years ago. Piecing together our past from the vestiges that have survived thousands of years challenges us to think about how we have arrived at where we are today . . .

We stood on top of the hill overlooking the broad valley. Below us were small spruce trees, stubby brush and a meandering creek. The far side of the valley was lined with low-lying hills, while in the distance you could see the snow-capped peaks of the St. Elias Mountains.

Norm Easton gestured south across the valley as he told me about the place where we were standing. It was an archeological site that according to carbon-dating was occupied at least 12,000 and possibly 14,000 years ago, making it the oldest in the southwest Yukon.

As we looked out across the valley, he explained that this was a natural vantage point to watch for game. Twelve thousand years ago, we would have been looking across a flat grass-covered plain. Herds of bison roamed across the expanse of land. Wapiti and caribou would have also dotted the landscape. Occasionally, large mammoth would lumber past. To the east and south the glaciers were slowly retreating.

This expanse represents a distant extension of the Tanana valley. Over in Alaska there are a number of well-documented sites of similar age. They contain tools of the same type and date that were found here. If you go any farther to the east, you reach a place where the water drains away to the Yukon River.

Because the valley constricts here, the game enter a natural funnel, making it an ideal vantage point for hunters. Humans have taken advantage of this site more or less continuously for the last 12,000 years. This could be the home of the earliest Canadians, though the people of long ago did not know or care about that. At that distant point in the past, they were part of the most easterly extension of a people occupying Beringia, an area encompassing most of Alaska and the western Yukon. Farther to the east was a gigantic mass of ice that stretched for thousands of kilometres, upon which it was impossible to live. To the west, these people could have travelled all the way to Siberia, which was connected to Alaska by a low-lying neck of land now referred to as the Bering Land Bridge. A few years into their future,

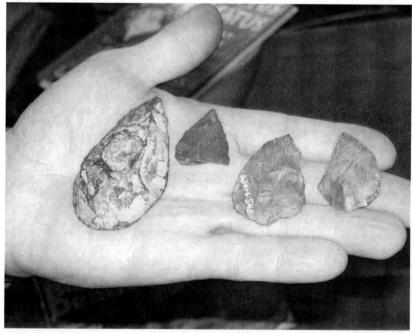

Archeologist Norm Easton holds in his hand some of the oldest clues to human occupation in Canada. MICHAEL GATES

the glaciers would melt and the oceans rise, covering this neck of land and separating North America from Asia.

Easton is an anthropologist, archeologist and instructor at Yukon College who has conducted research in this region for twenty years. Working with White River elders, he knows the history of the area as well as anyone. As we gaze over the valley before us, he explains how he came to conduct an archeological dig here.

Like many finds in archeology, the site was not discovered by design. Over the years, Easton had repeatedly camped on this very spot while hunting for moose. Back in 2001, he and a small crew were planning to conduct an archeological survey of the Scottie Creek Valley to the north but the weather wouldn't cooperate. It had been raining steadily for a week and Easton realized that even after it stopped it would be another week before the lowlands would be passable. Rather than have the crew idle, he instructed them to establish a series of test pits on the lookout. He was surprised by the abundance of artifacts uncovered over the next few days.

At the Little John site, archeologist Norm Easton describes the landscape as it looked more than 10,000 years ago. MICHAEL GATES

Easton named it the Little John site after an elder from the area, and with whose family he had hunted in this very place. The site is located within a stone's throw of the Alaska Highway and a short distance from the international boundary. Because four major archeological surveys had previously been conducted along the highway corridor, he had assumed there was nothing new to be found. The chance discovery in 2001 proved that you can't take anything for granted.

But there was an even bigger surprise in store for Easton, and it came from a most unlikely source.

The abundance of relics at the site, as well as its proximity to the highway, made this an excellent place to conduct an archeological field school in the following years. It was during this work in 2003 that Eldred Johnny, Little John's ten-year-old grandson, found a small teardrop-shaped stone tool at the site. Eldred presented it to Glen McKay, who quickly brought it to Easton's attention. This artifact changed everything. Extremely old and part of a tool tradition known as Nenana, or Chindadn, this represented the first occurrence of it to be found in Canada.

Easton has continued to excavate at the Little John site over subsequent years, and will be doing so again. Excavations at Little John have been conducted in several areas. Near the crest of the hill where the wind sweeps across the valley and up the slope to the site, soil deposits are very thin and artifacts dating back thousands of years can be found in close proximity to other stone tools of more recent vintage. Moving back from the edge of the hill the soil becomes much deeper and the separation between artifacts from different time periods becomes better defined. Farther back, in an area that Easton refers to as the Eastern Lobe, he has radiocarbon dates from a layer of wind-deposited silt (loess) of 14,000 years before the present.

In yet another portion of the site, known as the Swale Lobe, the deposits are over four metres deep. With any luck, this will produce cultural material from the earliest period of the site's occupation.

Easton gives much credit to the elders who have mentored him over the years, notably Tommy Johnny and the late Bessie John. He says that he has learned much from them that he can apply to his work. Stories told to the oldest surviving members of the White River First Nation when they were children refer to monstrous animals with big horns projecting out from their snouts. These stories were substantiated by recent work on the realignment of the Alaska Highway, which unearthed numerous mammal bones from the late Pleistocene era, including those of mammoths. The stories relating to these extinct creatures have been passed down through countless generations!

Work planned for the future will consist of a team of twenty-five people, including the University of Alaska Anchorage field school, specialists, students, members of the White River community, as well as those of Northway and Tetlin, Alaska. Work will include excavation, ethnobotany and ethnographic research, and Easton insists that his project activities also include community service in Beaver Creek.

If you are driving the highway to Alaska, you will find the site just a couple of kilometres from the international boundary. Stop for a unique glimpse of the some of the Yukon's earliest history being unearthed.

Dam History Forecasts Catastrophe on the Alsek

A presentation given by Jeff Bond in 2008 at the MacBride Museum revealed just how active the glacial history of the southwest Yukon has been over the past few thousand years . . .

"Then one time, you know, when my father's mother was a little girl up at Tinx kayani [. . . on the Tatshenshini], there was a flood all over. It was because my father's people made fun of a seagull. They threw it in the fire. It was a young one and couldn't fly. They threw it in again. All its feathers burned off. They laughed at it.

"And then a great flood came. And there was no place to be safe. That glacier broke that used to go across the Alsek."

—Emma Ellis, from an interview recorded
by Frederica De Laguna, August 5, 1952

That's how a resident of the Yakutat region of southeast Alaska described the cause and effect of the damming of the Alsek back in the 1800s. The Lowell glacier surged across the Alsek River Valley, blocking the Alsek River and creating a huge lake that went up the valley for many kilometres. Then the dam burst. A huge wall of water swept down the Alsek River to Dry Bay, causing carnage and death as it went.

Jeff Bond, surficial geologist with the Yukon Geological Survey, has been studying these events. The Alsek River has been blocked numerous times during the past few thousand years. The most recent events occurred around 1852 and 1909. Bond relates the flooding to the Little Ice Age, a period that spans several centuries from the 1400s till the 1800s. During that time, the temperature dropped a couple of degrees below what we now experience. It was enough to cause a dramatic shift in climate all over the world.

Prior to that period, the weather was warmer. The Norse settled Greenland, and the British grew grapes and produced wine that they exported to France. By the fifteenth century, however, things had turned colder. The Thames River froze over for the first time in 1408 and the Norse had

Looking north up the Alsek River . . . a glacial advance of a few hundred metres would result in the creation of a lake. AL VON FINSTER

abandoned Greenland. In the French Alps, glaciers began to advance. Old pictures of the Mer de Glace glacier at Chamonix, France, show it at a stage of advance in which an entire valley was filled with ice. That same valley today is ice-free. When the glacier made its maximum advance, it ground away farms and entire villages. One monstrous boulder can still be seen at the end of a glacial moraine, resting on the stone foundation of what was once a farmhouse. This is stark evidence of the havoc that results when one of these unstoppable ice rivers grinds its way down a valley. Imagine watching, year by year, as a massive wall of frozen water advances until it crushes your home into splinters!

Bond explored some explanations for this glacial activity in a presentation at the MacBride Museum of Yukon History in October 2008. A lack of sunspots is suggested as one cause. Sunspots increase the warmth from the sun, and Bond presented evidence that suggested that glacial surges could be related to periods when there was no such activity. (He also speculated that the recent absence of sunspots explained in part why we had such crummy weather in 2008.) Another possibility, he suggests, was volcanic activity. Cooling would be enhanced by increased atmospheric dust. Mount Tambora in Indonesia erupted in April 1815 in what is described as the largest such event in nearly 2,000 years. What followed was the "year without summer" (1816) that afflicted Europe and North America and resulted in summer frosts.

In his presentation Bond placed the village of Haines Junction in the geographical context of the Alsek River and the Lowell Glacier. The residual moraines along the hillsides where the Lowell Glacier enters the Alsek Valley are now high above the current-day ice and indicate how thick the glacier was during the Little Ice Age.

Just downstream from the Lowell Glacier is another glacier, the Tweedsmuir, which had advanced a few hundred metres in 2008. The US Geological Survey has a webcam monitoring the situation because of the potential damage to the Alaskan community in Dry Bay. Currently, there is only a narrow channel remaining at the glacial front through which the Alsek River flows. An advance of another hundred metres or so could dam the river and create a reservoir behind the ice.

Research funded by Foothills Pipeline in the 1980s facilitated a study of the lakes formed by different surges of the Lowell Glacier. Wave-cut shore-lines are visible for hundreds of metres up the hillsides of the Alsek valley, and tree-ring analysis of the driftwood along these old beaches has made it possible to place different events in time.

From this work, Bond showed graphic depictions of old shorelines along the Alsek and Dezadeash valleys in the area of Haines Junction. The deep-est lake in recent times was formed in the late 1400s at an elevation of 640 metres above sea level (the weather recording station at Haines Junction is at an elevation of 595 metres ASL). A later glacial advance in the early 1700s created a reservoir almost as deep; a third event, around 1852, formed a body of water at around 595 metres elevation. Other lesser episodes probably oc-curred during the Little Ice Age, however, evidence of these would have been washed away by subsequent damming.

Bond showed a series of modified Google images of the Haines Junction and Alsek River area that illustrated what these elevated water levels would do to the landscape. In the highest of the recent damming events, present-day Haines Junction was under water, and a lake extended up the Dezadeash Valley as far as Marshall Creek. During lesser episodes, Haines Junction would have been at least lakefront property.

While this paints a gloomy picture of the prospects for property owners in Haines Junction, it suggests even poorer fortunes are in store for people living downstream. Oral traditions of the First Nations tell of terrible floods with great loss of life that occurred down the Alsek Valley and into Dry Bay. Scientific evidence supports this. Bond showed pictures of giant ripples or flood dunes up to four metres high that give mute testimony to the violence of the flooding once the ice gave way. A wall of water many metres high sur-ging down the Alsek Valley would have been something to behold—and fear.

The traditional and scientific knowledge are both hard to ignore. If you ever plan to buy real estate at Haines Junction, think about a property up high with a good view.

Ice and Snow Yield Secrets of the Past

In the Yukon, we are blessed with more than our share of ice and snow. While they may be an inconvenience, forcing us to apply shoulder to shovel in an effort to keep our driveways clear in the winter, they also provide us with a glimpse into the past.

Every day I take the family dog for a walk in the woods. Eagerly, she sniffs each tree and snowbank, sometimes retrieving treasures of questionable origin. I think there must be some bloodhound in her family tree.

It is not as easy for archeologists to "sniff" out the remnants of early Yukon inhabitants; they must rely on visual acuity and experience gained from years of surveying the landscape in search of ancient remains. Unfortunately, there are only a few of these specialists in our territory, which is twice the size of Great Britain. We are a northern people and we know that snow and ice play an important role in the annual cycle of life. Our climatic characteristics combined with serendipity have been instrumental in providing us with some of the most interesting and exciting archeological discoveries in recent times.

In July 1991, David Hik, then a graduate student at the University of Alberta, was conducting research on little furry creatures called pikas in the southwest Yukon. This work took him to about as isolated a location as one could imagine in the St. Elias Mountains of Kluane National Park. On a rocky slope surrounded by ice and snow as far as the eye could see, he found a small fragment of animal skin. Hik brought this unusual find to Parks Canada staff in Haines Junction. When examined, it proved to be a 1,100-year-old piece of grizzly-bear hide that had been worked by human hands. The treasure was stabilized by conservators and is now kept in special environmentally controlled storage in the Parks Canada service centre in Winnipeg.

Imagine an early forefather of Yukon's indigenous people travelling with this simple bearskin artifact through some of the most forbidding country in the Yukon. At the same time, Vikings were sacking England, the Mayan Empire was waning in Central America, and the Sung Dynasty was being founded in China.

In 1997, wildlife-biologist Gerry Kuzyk and his wife Kristin Benedek were hunting in the mountains west of Kusawa Lake when they found something that would change our view of Yukon's past forever. Oozing out of a discoloured layer of melting snow was a dark stain. Closer examination revealed the source to be caribou dung. Since caribou hadn't frequented the

Parks Canada collection specialist Debbie Cochrane in Winnipeg displays a 1,100-year-old bearskin artifact from the icefields of Kluane National Park. MICHAEL GATES

area for seventy years, they collected a few pellets for analysis. They also discovered a small wooden artifact.

When these samples were radio-carbon dated, they proved to be thousands of years old. The wooden artifact was of particular interest to Yukon Government archeologist Greg Hare. Such items do not survive for long in the ground as the soil is acidic. Usually, only stone tools can resist these conditions. Here was a unique opportunity to study the Yukon's early inhabitants in a way that had never before been possible. Since that discovery, Hare, and a small First Nation research team from the six First Nations with ice patches in their traditional territories, have combed the hillsides of the southwest Yukon, locating dozens of similar ice patches. Some of the rare organic artifacts found at these sites date back 9,000 years.

These finds yield valuable new information about the lives of the Yukon's earliest residents. A careful analysis of the radio-carbon dates of the artifacts collected from these sites revealed that the hunting technology changed about 1,200 years ago from atlatl to bow and arrow. Atlatls are long sticks, about the length of your forearm, hooked at one end so that a long spear or dart can be launched from them. They give a mechanical advantage over hand-thrown spears, and allowed hunters to attack caribou, which would have climbed to these high-altitude snow patches to escape obnoxious insects, from a greater distance.

These Yukon finds, unique to the frozen conditions found in the north, created an opportunity for First Nation students to participate in the search for artifacts near these historic iceboxes. Imagine the exhilaration these researchers would have experienced as they found small weapons, thousands of years old, complete with stone points lashed to one end of a long wooden shaft, with sinew and feathers lashed onto the other. Perfectly preserved as though they had been fashioned yesterday!

In 1999, yet another fascinating discovery was made in the ice and snow near the southwest corner of the Yukon. Again, it wasn't made by archeologists, but by three schoolteachers from southern British Columbia who were hunting sheep in the vicinity of the Tatshenshini River. Warren Ward, Bill Hanlon and Mike Roch were walking on the rocks along the foot of a small glacier, or ice patch, when something caught their eye. Looking closely they found some carved pieces of wood and a patch of fur. Then they saw bones—human bones. After hiking for twenty hours to reach their truck, they drove to Whitehorse, where they reported their find to the staff at the Beringia Centre. Things went into high gear after that. The resulting discovery is now called Kwädąy Dän Ts'inchį, or "Long Ago Man Found." Kwädąy Dän Ts'inchį was transported, along with the artifacts found nearby, to the Royal British Columbia Museum in Victoria, BC, for study and conservation.

According to archeologist Sheila Greer, who spoke at a Land Claims Symposium sponsored by Yukon College, we know that somewhere between 1670 and 1850 AD, a young male of eighteen or nineteen years old was travelling into the interior from one of the Chilkat Tlingit villages on the coast (likely Klukwan or Kluktu) and perished from a cause undetermined but most likely exposure. We also know from the research that he had just departed from the coast on his way to the interior. While he had been in the interior for some time in the period before his death, his long-term home was on the coast. We now recognize, through DNA analysis, the identity of some of his living relatives, and that he was a member of the Wolf or Eagle moiety.

There are many more things we can learn about him, but even what has been revealed thus far is a fascinating glimpse of our human past. Mother Nature has provided us with an icy opportunity to glimpse into the looking glass of time.

Any one of us may find ourselves in a situation where we encounter something from the distant past. It's not always the trained professional who makes the significant finds, however they are clearly the ones who will help reveal the intriguing details that make our history come alive.

The next time you encounter something curious lying on the ground while out hiking, hunting or working on the land, make sure you report your discovery to your friendly neighbourhood archeologist.

THE EARLY DAYS

The Fortymile River Makes for Challenging History

The Fortymile River was a major component of my first book, Gold at Fortymile Creek. *Much to my chagrin, I was not able to travel over the river until after the book was written. As you make this exploration with me, you may be confused by the usage of Forty Mile and Fortymile. Forty Mile refers to the town and Fortymile to the river at whose mouth the townsite is located.*

The drone of the motorboat was muffled by the roar of the rapids as we negotiated the Cleghorn Riffle on the Fortymile River. This is a deceptive piece of the river where the water is churned into metre-high waves by the boulder-strewn channel. Larry Taylor, a veteran Alaskan guide and resident of the Fortymile, put us ashore to walk this stretch of the river while he navigated the 150 metres of whitecapped water. The pamphlet provided by the US Bureau of Land Management hadn't prepared us for the turbulence here, nor had it placed the riffle accurately on the map. Woe to the unsuspecting canoeist who would come around the bend in the river to confront this unfriendly water.

It was August 1998 and as a gold-rush centennial project, my friends Bill Berry, John Gould and I secured Larry's expertise to take us on a journey through time and space. We had great confidence in Larry's intimate

Only a few derelict cabins now remain to testify to the early days of mining on the Fortymile River. MICHAEL GATES

knowledge of the Fortymile River, which spans the Yukon–Alaska boundary down to the Yukon River northwest of Dawson City. Larry knew first-hand the dangers: on his first Fortymile trip many years before, he had lost everything going through a section of the river known as The Falls.

Bill, a retired California banker, was retracing the route of his ancestor Clarence J. Berry, who laboured up the Fortymile River to Franklin Gulch before the Klondike gold rush. I was curious to travel the route that I had described in my book *Gold at Fortymile Creek*. John, a historian from Dawson City, was there because of his natural curiosity and his voluminous knowledge of gold-mining history.

While never yielding the spectacular gold production of the Klondike River basin, the Fortymile was one of the most productive gold-bearing creeks discovered before the Klondike gold rush. The prospectors had given colourful names to every sandbar and tributary: Troublesome Point, Dogtown, Bonanza Bar, Wildcat Riffles, Deadman's Riffles and the Cleghorn. Every name had a story.

The adventure we were on was the most profound for Bill, I think. His great-uncle Clarence eked out a living mucking for gold on Franklin Gulch before the Klondike. To make ends meet, Clarence was reduced to tending bar for Bill McPhee in his saloon in the small cluster of log buildings where the Fortymile River meets the Yukon. McPhee grubstaked him, and he struck it rich on Eldorado Creek in the Klondike. Clarence repeated his luck at Fairbanks a few years later, and then trebled his good fortune when he invested in California oil.

But at the moment, the Cleghorn Riffle was on our mind. The early prospectors travelled this route by tracking or lining their goods upstream in boats. This demanding technique required at least two men, one to drag the supply-laden craft upstream with a rope while the other kept the stern out in the current with a long pole. The work was both tedious and exhausting. It took days to haul the cargo from the trading posts at the town of Forty Mile to Franklin Gulch, about 140 kilometres upriver.

We were laden with guilt: where the old-timers struggled for days against the current, often immersed in frigid water to their hips, we were making the same trip in a few hours in a motorboat. The early-day miners bivouacked on the banks of the river, battling weather and mosquitoes as they fought their way upstream. In contrast, each night we were transported back to the

Bill Berry and Larry Taylor pan for gold on a bar on the Fortymile River.
MICHAEL GATES

Taylors' tidy and comfortable home at O'Brien Creek, a tributary of the Fortymile, for a delicious home-cooked meal prepared by Larry's wife, June. After that, we could relax in the comfort of a sauna before retiring to one of the tidy cabins for a good night's sleep.

The early-day miners lived and laboured in extreme isolation: a round-trip exchange of correspondence could take up to eighteen months. Miners were so starved for news from the outside world that the newspaper wrapping in a parcel from Outside was literally worth its weight in gold.

The prospecting and mining work was all done by hand in those days. Three miners handsawed 50,000 feet of lumber for a flume to divert water a kilometre and a half from Franklin Gulch to their claim on Troublesome Point. Another partnership did the same, earning seventy-five dollars per day for their efforts, an excellent return on their investment for that time.

It was on the Fortymile that they perfected the technique of drift mining, which enabled a miner to thaw and dig his way down to bedrock through frozen ground in the winter. It was a dramatic improvement over remaining idle all winter while awaiting summer's return. Drift mining was later employed extensively in the Klondike.

In 2003, I took a second trip down the Fortymile in large inflatables with a team of cultural resource specialists. It had been a hot, dry summer. This time the water was so low in the upper portion of our journey that I waded across the main channel in rubber boots. We dragged our craft over numerous shallows and floated slowly along. At The Falls, where the river drops almost three metres in a short distance, we floated gently through. What a different experience from my previous journey when Larry Taylor navigated it at full throttle. We never did negotiate the most dangerous portion of all: the Canyon Rapids on the Canadian side of the border.

The Fortymile flows gently past a cabin at Long Bar. If you come ashore here, you will find a small memorial for two people who died in the Canyon Rapids around 1980. Two couples, one of whom lived in that cabin, tried to make it through the canyon during high spring runoff. One member of each couple lost their life, and the lovely log cabin at Long Bar, now abandoned, became a symbol of a spoiled dream.

Until the prospectors learned the stern code of the Fortymile, the river and its canyon took many lives. The year following the discovery of gold was particularly deadly. The first to drown was a prospector named Tom Jones, who was stranded on a boulder in the canyon only six metres from shore and tried to swim, thinking that he could reach it safely. He was caught in the deadly undertow and sucked below the frothing currents. After Jones, the toll quickly mounted and the names Lamont, Saffron, Johnson, Holmes and Wells were added to the death roll, but most tragic was the account of a Gwitchin man who, after capsizing in the canyon and mistakenly thinking that his entire family had perished, cut his own throat.

While encounters with the past are my main goal as a history hunter, safety remains paramount. After all, I'd like to be around to do it again.

The Force in the North: the First Mounties

This is the first in a series of three accounts about the first Mounted Police in the Yukon.

The Yukon was lawless in the early days. Before the arrival of the North-West Mounted Police in 1895, there was no centralized authority. In fact, until that time there was not a clearly defined boundary between the Yukon and Alaska, although its location on a map had long been determined.

In those days, the Yukon basin was occupied mainly by Americans even though the dividing line was officially the 141st meridian. Nevertheless, the Americans were of the opinion that if there was no one there to say where the boundary was, who was to say whether they were occupying their own soil or not?

The Canadian government was aware of this situation. However, in 1883 American army lieutenant Frederick Schwatka led a well-publicized military expedition through Canadian territory over the Chilkoot Pass and down the Yukon River. The Canadian government responded in 1887 by sending three survey parties into the Yukon. One of the groups, under the direction of surveyor William Ogilvie, travelled down the Yukon past Forty Mile to the general vicinity of the international border and spent the winter of 1887–88 surveying the area to determine the precise point where the boundary intersected the great river.

Nevertheless, the American traders at Forty Mile maintained that the town was on American soil. They even had an official US post office there masquerading under the name of Mitchell, Alaska. Further, it was the American practice to establish miners' committees and meetings to serve in the role of self-regulation, contrary to the Canadian law, where authority came from the Crown. Asserting Canada's sovereignty in the Yukon territory would become one of the primary roles of the Mounted Police when they arrived on the scene.

In 1893, Bishop William Bompas, the Anglican missionary posted in the tiny mining community of Forty Mile, wrote two letters to the Canadian government regarding the corrupting influence of the sale of liquor to the Natives of the area. He also documented violent incidents and called for the police and a customs authority to be sent in.

About the same time, C.H. Hamilton, assistant manager of the North American Transportation and Trading Company (NAT&T) at Fort Cudahy, wrote a similar letter. He recommended that a collector of customs, collector of internal revenue and police protection be established, and proposed that the expenses be recovered from the revenue generated from duty on imported goods. Any delay in doing so, he suggested, could result in a Native uprising.

The government responded by sending Inspector Charles Constantine and Staff Sergeant Charles Brown of the North-West Mounted Police to investigate. They were instructed to exercise their authority with discretion. The two left Victoria on June 22, 1894, and arrived at Forty Mile August 7, having followed the same route over the Chilkoot used by the miners. While in Forty Mile, Constantine gathered information about the situation there, and collected $3,248.88 in customs duties. He also verified that there was importation of liquor. Constantine departed for Outside a month later, leaving Sergeant Brown behind at Fort Cudahy, across the Fortymile River from the rough-and-ready log town of Forty Mile. For the next ten months, Brown was the only Canadian government representative in the Yukon.

During his stay, Brown witnessed a number of events that exposed the lawlessness in the miners' society. In December, a man named Sailer tried to shoot another named Frank Bowker but failed when someone knocked his gun off target as he pulled the trigger. Sailer was popular among the miners,

For a few years, Forty Mile was the largest community in the Yukon.
RCMP HISTORICAL COLLECTION, CATALOGUE NUMBER 1934.15.6

so nothing happened to him. Only the previous year, George Matlock and another man were involved in a similar incident. Illicit liquor production was rife. There was a "whiskey gang" comprised of a number of men, including Jack McQuesten and T.W. O'Brien. O'Brien later established the only brewery in Dawson City. Sergeant Brown was able to locate nearly thirty-five illicit stills operating in the region.

In January, Brown witnessed another event that suggested the need for law and order in the Yukon. At a miners' meeting in Fortymile, the committee decided that C.H. Hamilton, not a popular man among the miners, should compensate a servant girl he had fired. Hamilton did not offer the liberal credit that the miners had become accustomed to at Jack McQuesten's Forty Mile trading post. The mob threatened to blow up the company safe to get the funds if necessary. To avert violence, Sergeant Brown counselled Hamilton to pay up.

Over the winter, Brown also collected over $5,000 in duty on imported goods, mainly from the NAT&T Company. While getting good co-operation from the NAT&T, the same could not be said for trader Jack McQuesten across the river in Forty Mile, who successfully evaded the sergeant's efforts to collect duty from him. Sensing the winds of change, and not liking their direction, McQuesten was quick to move to the more friendly environment of his trading post at Circle, Alaska, 250 kilometres beyond the reach of the Mounted Police, in the spring of 1895.

Following Constantine's instructions, Sergeant Brown left Fort Cudahy June 20, 1895, and headed 1,000 kilometres west to St. Michael, Alaska, at the mouth of the Yukon River. Meanwhile, back in Ottawa, the Canadian government had decided to establish a detachment at Forty Mile, with Inspector Constantine in charge. Although Constantine had urged that a force of forty men would be required, he was given twenty, including Inspector D'Arcy Strickland, assistant surgeon A.E. Wills, two staff sergeants, two corporals and thirteen constables, recruited in early 1895. Constantine and his contingent departed Regina on June 18, 1895. Five days later, they embarked from Seattle on the steamship *Excelsior*, headed for Unalaska and St. Michael.

Within days, the *Excelsior* was jammed in floe ice in the Bering Sea off St. Lawrence Island. Hemmed in on all sides by endless sheets of ice, the hapless Mounties had to wait days before they were freed from their icy prison. On July 3 they arrived at St. Michael, where Sergeant Brown joined them, and they all left two days later on the *Portus B. Weare*, the twin-stacked river steamer of the NAT&T Company.

Two years later, the *Excelsior* delivered the first gold-laden Klondike miners to San Francisco, thus sparking the gold rush.

The trip upriver against the powerful Yukon current was slow and tedious and punctuated by frequent stops for firewood. The journey became a monotonous cruise plagued by unbearable (and unusual) heat and dense clouds of fierce northern mosquitoes that reached their worst at Fort Yukon. The squad arrived at its destination at Fort Cudahy on July 24 and immediately upon unloading their supplies set about establishing the first Mounted Police post in the Yukon.

The Mounted Police were well positioned and prepared for the events that would unfold over the next two years.

The Mounted Police in Forty Mile

One tends to think of the early Mounted Police as heroic figures overseeing the development of the north. While Sergeant Preston was outwitting a villain every week on the long-running radio program, in real life the role of the Mounted Police was not as exciting as it was made out to be . . .

Upon their arrival at the mouth of the Fortymile River in July 1895, the Mounted Police immediately became beasts of burden, dragging and hauling tons of supplies from where they had been unceremoniously dumped in a disorganized jumble on the riverbank. Inspector Constantine, now the commanding officer, selected the site of the new police post. It was to occupy the ground that lay strategically between the NAT&T Company post at Fort Cudahy, which was a short distance downriver, and the disorganized array of log cabins at Forty Mile on the opposite side of the mouth of the Fortymile River.

What despair these men must have felt when they gazed upon what was to become their new home: a scattering of stunted spruce trees on ground covered with a spongy, saturated layer of moss forty centimetres thick!

On July 26, construction began. Constantine sent a squad of nine men led by Inspector Strickland fifty kilometres upriver on the steamer *Portus B. Weare* to the mouth of the Twelve Mile River. For three weeks, under primitive conditions and enduring the vicious attacks of swarms of mosquitoes, Strickland's men cut and lugged, by hand, 400 logs to the shore of the Yukon. The timber was bound together to form three large rafts and floated downriver to Fort Cudahy.

Meanwhile Inspector Constantine and the remainder of the men were busy preparing the ground upon which the newly named Fort Constantine barracks were to be built. Bush had to be cleared and drains built to draw off excess water. The thick surface moss was stripped away.

"All entailed much hard work and was gone on with regardless of the state of the weather," reported Constantine. "If it was not ninety degrees in the shade, it was pouring rain. At any time the men were working up to their ankles and sometimes up to their knees in water."

Constantine rented the sawmill from the NAT&T Company and when the party returned from upriver with the log rafts, they set about cutting the logs. A wooden tramway was built from the sawmill to the post, a distance of 500 metres, to make the task of transporting the freshly sawn lumber easier. All of the construction work was completed by the officers and men with no outside help.

Fort Constantine was laid out in a quadrangle consisting of eight

The building of Fort Constantine is underway. RCMP HISTORICAL COLLECTION, CATALOGUE NUMBER 1934.15.6

A dog team pulls a plow to prepare the ground for the construction of Fort Constantine. RCMP HISTORICAL COLLECTION, CATALOGUE NUMBER 1934.15.6

buildings lining the perimeter of a small parade square. It was contained within a stockade, essentially a wall of close-packed posts that spanned the spaces between the buildings and completed the front of the enclosure. The buildings consisted of a guardroom, barracks, storehouse and office, hospital, quarters for two officers, the surgeon and the staff sergeants. Bastions three metres to a side were constructed at opposite corners of the stockade. The entrance and fifteen-metre flagpole faced the river.

The work was completed and the men moved into the barracks October 7, followed a week later by the officers who settled with their families into separate quarters. Sergeant Hayne summed it up: "Those [buildings] that we now erected were naturally more elaborate than the ordinary run of buildings ... for they were destined to a degree of permanency for which the miner's 'shack' is never intended, and as far as we could, we studied comfort and convenience. Seeing that we had to live there for two years and then be succeeded in two years by others in the same quarters.

"Our life, too, had to be very different from that of the miners. We had all our regular apparatus for cooking and washing, work (clerical and

Inspector D'Arcy Strickland supervises the milling of lumber for construction of Fort Constantine. YUKON ARCHIVES, D'ARCY EDWARD STRICKLAND FONDS, PHOTO YA 09394

manual) and recreation. We had to keep ourselves clean and tidy. In a word, we had to aim at erecting as near a model as was possible under the circumstances of a decent civilized set of barracks, in which we should be able to conform to the more important of the requirements of discipline and civilization."

At the time, the North-West Mounted Police were more like a military force than are the RCMP of today. The men lived together in an encampment, following a rigid and disciplined routine. Reveille was at 06:20 a.m., the morning roll call followed at 7:00 a.m., and "lights out" was at 11:00 p.m. The routine included watch-setting roll, kit inspections and maintenance of arms. The men were to be kept proficient in squad and arms drill. Orders were issued for revolver target practice. A special routine was observed on Sundays.

With the onset of winter, the men were required to consume a daily dose of lime juice to prevent scurvy, a scourge whose prevention was still not widely understood by the neighbouring miners.

Records show that conduct was good but there were occasional infractions and penalties for misuse of weapons, sleeping in, unauthorized absences, insubordination and drunkenness.

If the men volunteered because they thought their northern assignment would bring them adventure, they must have been sadly disappointed. The call for survival was louder and far more forceful. That year freeze-up occurred on October 17, and by December and all through January, the temperatures had fallen from minus twenty degrees Celsius, to minus fifty-five. The detachment consumed two cords of wood daily in the cold weather, and all men, with the exception of mess cook, carpenter and orderly, went on general fatigue two days a week to cut their wood supply and haul it to the fort. Occasional patrols by dogsled were the only relief from the monotony, with miners greeting them peacefully; once the location of the international boundary was established, the Mounties also inspected mining activity in Canadian territory and collected mining royalties.

As the spring of 1896 arrived, the urgency to keep warm was replaced with the need to keep dry. The barracks leaked constantly during the heavy rains of the spring and summer that year. Oil sheets and tarpaulins were placed over all the beds.

Mindful of the demand for an ample supply of dry firewood for the coming winter, Constantine sent patrols out in search of a reliable source. Wood was difficult to find and only an island eighty kilometres up the Yukon had enough to supply them with a hundred cords.

Ironically, the location where the men cut the wood for a new recreation room was at the mouth of the Klondike River, soon to be the home for thousands of gold-crazed stampeders.

Showdown on Glacier Creek

For those first Mounties posted to the Yukon, the challenges were many but the criminals were few. Establishing the police post at the mouth of the Fortymile River served a purpose greater than simply apprehending bad guys; it was an opening scene in a larger drama about to unfold . . .

The first case brought before Inspector Constantine occurred on August 25, 1895, only a month after the arrival of the North-West Mounted Police. D.W. Walker accused J.A. Williams of bringing stolen goods into Canada. The "stolen goods" in question turned out to be the affections of Walker's wife. Williams was at the altar of Bishop Bompas, the Anglican missionary at Forty Mile, when he was arrested by Sergeant Hayne and taken into custody at Fort Constantine.

At the time of the arrest, the post was still under construction, so there was no proper guardroom or jail in which to detain him. Given the physical state of the facilities, and the difficulty in obtaining sufficient evidence for a conviction, Williams was allowed to escape custody and flee downriver by boat.

A few months later, in December, Gus Clements was convicted of selling liquor to an aboriginal man and fined one hundred dollars plus costs. In March of 1896, a second charge of theft against Mr. Clements was dismissed. Two other men were fined five dollars or thirty days hard labour for breach of the peace, while a third was penalized by one hundred dollars or two months hard labour once again for selling liquor to an aboriginal man.

These infractions seem insignificant, considering the cost of maintaining a force of twenty officers and men in the far reaches of the new dominion of Canada, but the North-West Mounted Police were soon to confront a situation that would test their mettle and firmly establish their authority once and for all.

It all came about because of a miners' meeting. Once held in high regard, the miners' meetings had over the years deteriorated to the point where they were considered by some as nothing short of a farce. This was due to the population increasing and becoming more diverse, and because of the

The first Mounties in the Yukon had to maintain an air of civilization in contrast with the rough-and-ready miners of Forty Mile. RCMP HISTORICAL COLLECTION, CATALOGUE NUMBER 1934.15.6

influence of liquor and the presence of women. Saloons had become the centres of the gold-mining communities along the Yukon River and were a potent factor in the social change taking place.

According to William Ogilvie, a government surveyor who was a resident of Forty Mile and witness to the changes occurring in the community, "Like saloons everywhere else, they had their clientele of loafers, and like all the tribe, they interfered with other people's business more than they attended to their own.

"After the establishment of the saloons, miners' meetings were often held in them, and as all present were generally counted miners, . . . only some were so when they had to be, seeing it was the only means of employment in the country, so all had a vote."

The problems with the miners' committee is illustrated in the case of French Joe, who on a trip down the Fortymile River to town obliged a miner he passed by taking two ounces of gold from him to give to Bill Smith. French Joe made the delivery as promised but Smith complained that the unnamed miner who asked Joe to deliver his gold owed him an additional ounce, and demanded that French Joe produce it. Joe refused, having delivered all he had been given, so Smith called a miners' meeting in Bob English's saloon. Eighty-six men listened to the case and voted in favour of French Joe supplying the ounce of gold in question, in addition to paying twenty dollars for the rental of the saloon and buying drinks for the house. The amount totalled one hundred dollars, a large penalty for someone simply doing a favour for a stranger.

Trader and founder of Dawson City, Joe Ladue once lamented that ". . . nobody can get justice from a miners' committee when women [are] on one side." The small number of women trickling into the territory had a significant impact on the conduct of miners in their meetings, such as with the incident of C.H. Hamilton's servant girl (described earlier in "The Force in the North: the First Mounties"), or the infamous "coon" trial in Circle, Alaska. In the latter case, liquor was involved, and the proceedings were seen as more of a prank than true justice. Because of these and other similar incidents, the miners' committee and the Mounties were on a collision course, and that collision occurred in June 1896.

A man had leased Claim Number "19 Above Discovery" on Glacier

The first Mounted Police detachment in the Yukon consisted of twenty officers and men. Inspector Constantine is standing fourth from the left. YUKON ARCHIVES, D'ARCY EDWARD STRICKLAND FONDS, PHOTO YA9387

Creek in the nearby Sixtymile district from its owners. In the spring he defaulted on payment of his workers and skipped the country. A miners' committee then decided that it was up to the two owners of the claim, Van Wagoner and Hestwood, to make good on the outstanding debt. Further, the committee took the claim from the owners to sell it off to the highest bidder in order to pay the amount owed by the lessee. Van Wagoner and Hestwood protested to Inspector Constantine, who advised the committee in writing on June 19 that their actions were illegal. The committee disregarded Constantine's warning, and sold the claim to a miner named Terry Baker. When Constantine refused to register the transfer of title, Baker stormed out of Forty Mile "breathing defiance and saying that the miners would see him through."

Constantine sent Inspector Strickland and a force of twelve, armed with pistols and Lee-Metford rifles, to Glacier Creek with orders to settle the dispute. After a day and a half of hard travel, the heavily armed Mounties arrived at Glacier Creek. They occupied the disputed claim, ejected Baker's agent, and refused to negotiate with the committee. After two days, the miners caved in without a shot being fired.

Those who felt their democratic rights had been violated retreated to Circle, on the American side of the border, where the miners' committee still ruled supreme. The Mounted Police, having settled the issue of who governed in Canadian territory, returned to the relatively quiet and humdrum task of maintaining law and order in the Yukon Valley.

The serenity was to be short-lived, however, and nothing would ever be mundane again for the men in uniform. Late in August, an American named George Washington Carmack stepped into Inspector Constantine's office at the Mounted Police post to announce that he would like to file a discovery claim on a little stream upriver. A tributary of the Klondike called Rabbit Creek, it would soon be renamed Bonanza!

Frederick Schwatka's Forgotten Expedition

I chose to write about this aspect of Frederick Schwatka's Yukon explorations because while his 1883 journey down the Yukon River is well publicized, his second expedition was almost lost to history . . .

If you have heard of Frederick Schwatka, it is probably because of his famous Yukon River trip of 1883. Readers may not know that eight years later he returned to the Yukon for a second, less-publicized expedition.

His first trek through the Yukon was a reconnaissance project sponsored by the United States Army, the purpose of which was to assess the military capacity of the indigenous population. One of the legacies of the 1883 journey was that Schwatka named practically every landmark he encountered after one of his social connections as a means of currying favour. Bennett Lake, named after an American newspaper publisher, and Miles Canyon, honouring a US army general, are two examples of Schwatka's attempts to ingratiate himself to influential colleagues.

Schwatka had an interesting but short career. Born of Polish immigrant parents, he graduated from West Point military college in 1871 with the rank of second lieutenant in the United States Army. He was an intelligent man and in 1875, through his own initiative and study, was admitted to the bar in the district of Nebraska. The following year, he received a degree in medicine. He was assigned to the US Cavalry on the central plains and participated in the campaigns against the Sioux under General George Crook. In 1876, he engaged in battles at Tongue River, the Rosebud and Slim Buttes, but fortunately for him and for Yukon history, not at Little Bighorn.

His first taste of exploration came when he was seconded from the army in 1878 to join an arctic expedition sponsored by the American Geographical Society in search of the ill-fated Sir John Franklin, who perished while searching for the Northwest Passage. The two-year expedition found evidence of the tragic demise of Franklin's party. In the process, Schwatka earned a reputation as an arctic explorer. Three years later, under instructions from

Frederick Schwatka was essentially an American officer spying in Canadian territory when he made his first voyage (1883) to the Yukon. *A SUMMER IN ALASKA*, FREDERICK SCHWATKA, 1891

General Nelson Miles, he was dispatched to the Yukon River basin in a semi-official expedition through Canadian territory to determine the military strength of Alaskan Natives.

With the Indian Wars slowly coming to an end and career opportunities limited in the military, Schwatka resigned his commission and cashed in on the notoriety gained from his arctic experiences. He wrote books, most notably *A Summer in Alaska*, and lectured on his experiences to eager audiences across the United States.

Three years later, in 1886, Schwatka attempted another Alaskan exploration. This time, he planned to climb Mount St. Elias, but due to ill health and poorer physical condition, this journey ended in failure. Schwatka had mixed success in subsequent campaigns to the Yellowstone region and the Sierra Madre Mountains of Mexico. Badly overweight, his reputation flagging, he desperately needed another successful venture to bolster his career. In 1891 he was able to convince John Wesley Powell, the head of the US Geological Survey, to have C. Willard Hayes, a rookie geologist, accompany him on an expedition to the White and Copper River areas, sponsored by the *New York Ledger*.

That summer the duo headed north to Juneau, and with the guidance of an experienced prospector named Mark Russell followed the Taku River route to Teslin Lake and thus down the Teslin River to the Yukon (then called the Lewes) to Fort Selkirk. From the fort, the trio engaged a number of local Native guides, then set off on foot to the White River region in the southwest corner of the Yukon territory, then down the Copper River to the Alaska coast. They cut across country over hilly terrain, crossing streams and encountering an occasional group of local residents encamped at key fishing spots. When they arrived at the base of Mount St. Elias, they skirted along the edge of the glaciers, and three members of the group pushed through over the Skolai Pass and downstream to the Copper River.

The plan, after the expedition was completed, was for Dr. Hayes to document the formal scientific findings of their journey, while Schwatka would write a popular account for the newspapers and perhaps another book. Hayes's version included the first geologic reports of the Taku River area, and a route from Fort Selkirk to the Chitina River in Alaska. His was the first technical report describing the native copper deposits at the head of the White River. Anticipating Schwatka's own accounts of the journey, he mentioned little about his travelling companions.

Schwatka penned a series of articles published in the *New York Ledger* in 1892, but any plans for a book never materialized. Plagued by failing health and alcohol and morphine addiction, and demoralized by a disappointing speaking tour, it is believed he committed suicide by taking an overdose of laudanum. His body was found slumped in a doorway in Portland, Oregon, November 2, 1892.

Schwatka's account of this journey slipped into obscurity. It wasn't until 1996 when retired forester Arland Harris tracked down the accounts in the short-lived *New York Ledger* that Schwatka's last adventure became widely publicized.

Within a few weeks of the passage of Schwatka's group through the Nisling River country south and west of Fort Selkirk, another exploring party consisting of E.J. Glave (of Stanley Expedition fame) and Jack Dalton came across Schwatka's trail. Embarrassed by not being the first white man to reach this remote part of the Yukon, Glave did not report the encounter in his publications—just one more reason Schwatka's travels remained hidden from public awareness.

Dalton and Glave almost perished in the tempestuous waters of Kluane Lake that summer, but their survival helped prove the feasibility of using the Chilkat Pass to bring pack horses over the mountains into the interior. These two men were aware of the potential opportunities for mineral wealth well before the Klondike gold rush. It was Dalton, who, in 1898, brought noted mining engineer and entrepreneur Henry Bratnober to the White River, hoping to find a source of copper that could be developed for mining. They returned to the coast bearing fourteen kilograms of copper nuggets, some of them fist-sized.

Aside from producing quantities of native copper, the mining potential of the White River area never came to anything. In front of the MacBride Museum in Whitehorse, however, at the corner of First and Steele, you can still see prominently displayed one of the largest copper nuggets ever found, at 1,175 kilos. In 1958 it took five days for a team of six men using heavy equipment and the help of the Canadian Army to haul the slab from the White River to the Alaska Highway.

Tom Williams' Golden Death March

I believe this is one of the earliest examples of someone undertaking a dangerous journey in the name of gold—and losing his life in the process.

Howard Franklin and Henry Madison discovered coarse gold on what became known as Franklin's Bar, on the Fortymile River in the fall of 1886. What followed was one of the epic journeys in the history of the quest for gold in the Yukon.

At Fort Nelson, at the mouth of the Stewart River, trader Arthur Harper upon hearing of the new discovery realized that when news of the strike on the Fortymile River reached the Outside, there would be a stampede of substantial proportions. Harper's partner Jack McQuesten was in San Francisco making arrangements for next year's shipment of goods. Not knowing about this new turn of events, McQuesten could not possibly order enough supplies to deal with the anticipated flood of people.

Harper wrote a letter to McQuesten describing the new discovery and advising him to increase his order of supplies. Tom Williams, one of the miners wintering at Fort Nelson, volunteered to carry the message to the head of navigation at Dyea on the Alaskan coast where it could be forwarded to McQuesten. The other miners at the settlement quickly scribbled their own notes about the discovery for Williams to carry to friends back in civilization.

No prospector had ever before attempted to leave the Yukon during the winter. The journey he faced was formidable: a trek to the coast in the dark of winter over a distance of 1,000 kilometres with no trail to follow. Departing on December 1 with a dog team and a young Native man named Bob, Williams had little idea of the hardships ahead. Even if he had known, so determined was he to reach Dyea with his important messages that he would not have turned back.

The trip started easily enough. The weather that winter was the mildest in years and at first Tom and Bob covered up to forty kilometres every day. After a week, rain slowed them down. Travelling along the river, they encountered heavy pack ice, massive blocks frozen into contorted shapes, creating a grossly irregular surface over which only by heavy physical effort could they force the dogs and the sled full of supplies and letters forward.

At the end of the second week, after passing Rink Rapids, the sled broke and they had to stop to repair it. The following day, they travelled over ice covered with water. This was very hard on the dogs' paws, and slowed them down even more.

The warm weather weakened the ice. On December 17, Bob broke through it into water over his head. The same thing happened the next day, and the day after that. On the nineteenth the floe ice in the open water in the Yukon jammed, causing the water to rise. They received yet another dunking. Encountering more open water, the two men, now pushing an exhausted team, had to portage three kilometres through riverbank brush to reach more solid river ice. On December 22, they travelled only fourteen kilometres.

It was on this leg of the trip down the Yukon River that the two determined men encountered some bar miners wintering over along the upper Yukon. Tom and Bob were able to replenish their supplies while passing on the word of the new discovery, and collecting more letters to take Outside.

They pressed on, encountering more open water and warm weather. They were forced to travel along the shelf of ice that shouldered the watercourse. Then the weather turned bitterly cold as they forged ahead to the coastal mountain barrier. They arrived at Lake Laberge on New Year's Eve without celebration. Over the smooth lake ice, they made better time, but so obsessed were they with their goal they refused to rest. By this time, they were feeding their dogs from the rapidly dwindling supply of flour.

Both men and dogs were reaching total exhaustion as they moved up the Whitehorse Rapids, now ringed with fairy frost from the spray of the swiftly moving water. They continued past Miles Canyon, and trekked along the string of lakes at the headwaters of the Yukon. There they advanced over the smooth lake ice, making excellent mileage every day until they reached Bennett Lake where they encountered a band of wandering Natives whom they could not persuade to accompany them over the Chilkoot Summit. Ignoring warnings about the treacherous coastal pass, Williams and his young companion continued, encountering a violent blizzard. Fighting a strong headwind, they struggled for another thirty-two kilometres before the weather became so bad they could not move at all.

Tom and Bob negotiated another sixteen kilometres through heavy snow, then camped in the middle of Lake Lindeman without fuel or shelter from the storm.

The hardship continued. They abandoned their sled and began packing supplies on their backs. One exhausted dog could not continue so they abandoned it. They traversed eight kilometres in two days, then camped on the second day in a perpetual mountain storm. Finally, exhausted and out of food, they reached Stone House, below the Chilkoot summit. Somewhere along the trail, they had lost the last of their dogs, as well as the precious mail they were taking to the coast.

They were trapped for five days in a snow shelter at the foot of the coastal palisade without fire or food other than a little dry flour. Williams was sick and feverish with pneumonia when they emerged from their shelter on the sixth day. Leaving everything behind them, they struck out through the snow for Dyea. After only a short distance Williams collapsed and young Bob struggled on heroically through a metre of snow and a blinding blizzard with Williams on his back. They made only nineteen kilometres in five days. Luckily they encountered a wandering band of Chilkats who took them the remaining seven kilometres to Healy and Wilson's post at Dyea on the shore of Lynn Canal.

The trip was too much for Williams. He died within two hours of arriving at Dyea, but not before he told the astonished party at the store of the new discovery of gold. Wilson, the trader, sent out a party to find the mail pouch but they were driven back by the raging storm. A few days later,

J.J. Healy, Wilson's partner, arrived at Dyea. Young Bob and the electrifying announcement of the strike were quickly transported down the Pacific coast to Juneau.

Everyone in the coastal outpost was curious to discover what motivated the two men to undertake such a dangerous journey. Young Bob, picking up a handful of beans remarked: "Gold all same like this." That was the beginning of the first stampede to the Yukon in search of gold.

Later that winter Healy led another expedition into the pass to find the bundle of letters containing news of the strike, and a map. Beneath snowy peaks they found the mailbag, faithfully guarded by the last of Williams' dogs, dead and long frozen.

THE KLONDIKE
GOLD RUSH

Death on the Chilkoot Trail

This is a project I was involved in prior to retiring from Parks Canada.
I found its impact so profound at a personal level that I came back as a
volunteer to complete the work . . .

Steve Cassidy and I struggled out of the brush to get a clear view of Windy Arm. And there it was: a grave. You find the most unusual things as you hike through the northern wilderness, but still you don't expect to find someone buried in the middle of nowhere.

We had spent the day trekking back to Windy Arm from Tutshi Lake. Steve and I were conducting an archeological survey for the BC government along the route of the future road to Skagway. It was 1973 and the bulldozer sat at the BC border waiting for me to give consent to start clearing.

The dead man's name, J.F. Whitcomb, was inscribed on the metal plaque mounted on a large chunk of granite at the south end of an arm of Tagish Lake. I later found the Mounted Police report stating the cause of death. It was one of those tragic accidents that often occur: he was on the trail to the Klondike May 25, 1898, when he stumbled and his gun discharged. That was the end of his Klondike story. But the plaque mounted on the boulder remains to remind an occasional visitor of Whitcomb's demise.

During the gold rush, this story was repeated many times along the trail north to the Klondike. Resting on a sandy hillside behind the abandoned town of Bennett, BC, is a graveyard filled with the bodies of stampeders who died on their quest for gold. On a rocky terrace overlooking the former site of Lindeman City is another resting place with a dozen permanent residents sharing a magnificent view of Lindeman Lake. There are also individual graves scattered along the Chilkoot Trail.

These hopefuls came from all over Canada and the United States; others came from England. Both genders are represented, and young and old. Baby Henry Bluth died at Bennett on May 14, 1898. I imagine his parents were about to push their boat off on their way to Dawson City when the tragedy

Bennett, the terminus of the Chilkoot Trail, was a bustling place in the spring of 1898. Some Klondike stampeders died here. YUKON ARCHIVES, SCHARSCHMIDT FONDS, PHOTO YA 05636

The cemetery at Lindeman City on the Chilkoot Trail before restoration. MICHAEL GATES

occurred. At Lindeman City, the seven-month-old infant of Mr. and Mrs. Card died in May of 1897. The infant daughter of Mr. and Mrs. J.D. McKay also died and was laid to rest next to the Card child. A picket fence was built to protect the site. A hundred years later, the site that I believe contains these infant graves is located on a segment of the original trail now hidden from the thousands of hikers who pass by the vicinity each summer. The fence, long since collapsed and recently replaced with a replica to mark the site as part of a cemetery-restoration project, reminds us of the heartbreaking loss at this isolated spot.

The remains of Constable Pearson of the North-West Mounted Police are buried in the cemetery at Bennett. A new marker was placed on this site by the RCMP in 1998 to remind us of one, who in the service of those on their way north, was stricken with typhoid and died on August 30, 1898. Five railway workers are remembered in this cemetery, their names inscribed on a marble headstone.

I was able to account for at least seventy people buried or who had died along the trail within what is now the Chilkoot Trail National Historic Site.

These people died from drowning, freezing, typhoid, fire and avalanche. Two were known to have committed suicide. One of them, J.W. Mathes, attempted twice to float his supplies through the short stretch of rapids connecting Lindeman and Bennett Lakes. After losing his second outfit to the white water, he took his own life. Ironically, he is buried on a hillside overlooking, for eternity, the rapids that brought about his demise.

James McCue, from Hutchinson, Minnesota, was on his way home from Dawson City. The sixty-three-year-old blacksmith reached Bennett only to die alone of heart disease on a cold October day in 1898. He left behind a wife and eight children and possessions consisting only of forty-eight dollars in cash and five dollars' worth of nuggets.

Special thanks go to Ed and Star Jones, well-known Yukon-history researchers from Santa Fe, New Mexico, who have just completed a voluminous study of deaths in the Yukon, and to Parks Canada patrol person Christine Hedgecock for her extensive knowledge of the history of the trail. With their combined expertise we were able to locate and correctly identify one of the gravesites at Lindeman as that of Joseph Fortin, a relative of famed-pioneer Emilie Tremblay. Fortin died at Lindeman in 1894, three years before the stampede began.

The cemetery at Lindeman City on the Chilkoot Trail after restoration.
MICHAEL GATES

As part of my work, I have been able to add names to the growing list of souls who died unexpectedly on the Chilkoot Trail between the summit and Bennett. Most tragic of all are those whose identities have been lost to time. Often found with little or no identification, these individuals lie along the trail in simple unnamed graves.

Fortuitously, I was able to put a name to one unidentified individual. Buried in Lindeman cemetery, his marker had suffered the ravages of time. The wafer-thin cedar panel upon which his name had been inscribed had literally fallen apart from exposure to the elements. The inscription was barely legible. All that we could discern was that this person was from Aberdeen, Washington, was a member of the Masonic order, and that his last name included the letter "n". In candlelight in late August 2006, in the warden station at Lindeman Lake, Christine Hedgecock, park warden Rene Rivard and I scrutinized the shadows cast by the slightly raised letters of the weathered fragments of the panel, hoping to gain the identity of this individual, but to no avail.

I contacted Dann Sears, the director of the Aberdeen Museum of History the following winter. Within days, he responded to my query with some solid information. The June 2, 1898, edition of the *Aberdeen Herald* reported on this unfortunate death. His name was William S. Kent and he had died of typhoid fever May 16, 1898. Kent was a steam engineer who had worked for a number of years in a mill in Aberdeen before being caught up in the frenzy of the gold-rush stampede. Only two months earlier he and a friend had left Aberdeen in search of their fortune. Kent left a widow in Aberdeen to mourn his loss.

Having learned his identity and with the financial support of Masonic Lodge members from Whitehorse, we placed a new marker on his grave in August 2007. Overlooking the peaceful waters of Lindeman Lake I stood for a moment with park warden Simon Johnson beside Kent's grave. The day was bright and warm, and the air still as we paid our respects to the fallen prospector. William Kent's identity would now survive the passage of time.

Tagish Post was a Major Klondike Stop

Picture the Klondike gold seekers coming down the river in the thousands. During the gold rush, the waters of the Yukon River were the territory's lifeblood, and the stampeders were its pulse. Tagish Post was just one of a string of Mounted Police posts set up along the Trail to the Klondike to keep the stampeders safe . . .

As they coursed along the Yukon River, the stampeders made a stop at Tagish Post, on the north end of Tagish Lake, to check for mail, or register a claim. The outpost was a hint of civilization in what was to most of the newcomers a brutal, unforgiving wilderness.

At Tagish, they also registered with the North-West Mounted Police. Each boat or raft was painted with a number, and against that number, carefully inscribed in ledgers, were the names of the passengers. Just in case . . .

At the post, Tagish Lake constricts into a long neck that flows into Marsh Lake. On the east side of the channel were dozens of boats pulled up along the shore, which rose to a low terrace overlooking the water. The edge of the terrace was dotted with small white canvas tents, and in the centre of it all, a neat and impressive quadrangle of log buildings was built by the North-West Mounted Police to house the detachment of nearly fifty officers. The terrace was a hive of activity, with men moving to and fro, sharing news from Dawson and desperately seeking reports from the Outside, reporting to the

Mounties and checking their craft to ensure the precious cargoes of supplies were safe and dry. When mail was laid out on the ground in the middle of the open square, a mob clustered around in hopes of finding letters from home. This was a significant stop, but one of many, on the way to the Klondike.

Today the Tagish site is abandoned. In the summer of 2008, 110 years later, my young friend Pete Dunn and I approached the site not from the water as the stampeders did, but from a rough, narrow, twisting dirt road. When we arrived we were greeted from within the confines of an enclosed canopy of mosquito-proof nylon mesh by a crew of archeologists breaking for lunch. The mosquitoes swarmed around us, the biggest horde of the little biting creatures I had encountered all summer, making me thankful for the generous layer of bug dope I had applied before stepping out of the car.

We were welcomed by Victoria Castillo, the project's head archeologist, her husband, Grant Zazula, and their three-month-old son, Roman (the youngest archeologist on the crew). Rae-Ann Sidney and Austin Smith, both students from Carcross, completed the team.

As we talked between sandwiches, Ms. Castillo provided me with an overview of the project they are working on. Sponsored by the territorial

The North-West Mounted Police Post at Tagish must have been a formidable sight for stampeders who passed it during the gold rush.
YUKON ARCHIVES, ANTON VOGEE FONDS, PHOTO YA 00175

Archeologist Victoria Castillo is plotting the remains that survive at the site of the old Mounted Police Post at Tagish. MICHAEL GATES

government and the Carcross–Tagish First Nation, they were engaged in their second year of recording and testing of the former gold-rush destination. The previous year, they plotted the layout of the remains at the site. These consist mainly of scattered clusters of cast-off rusting tin cans and the rectangular mounds of sod that were once stacked up against the outer walls of more than two dozen log buildings. This year, the archeologists were refining and adding to their records.

Many of the buildings were eventually disassembled, and moved to Whitehorse. After the initial stampede, the White Pass and Yukon Route railroad reached Whitehorse from the coast in 1900. The river route was then abandoned almost overnight. The detachment was reduced to three men, and then closed down entirely around 1905.

The earth mounds and countless rusting cans are testimony to the events of more than a century ago. Ms. Castillo, who was completing her Ph.D. at the University of Alberta, patiently walked me through the dense undergrowth and showed me what they have found.

Of the original buildings, only two are still standing and their history may or may not be connected with the Mounted Police's use of the site. The rest of the site is camouflaged amidst spruce and pine trees and leafy willow branches. With a keen eye, you can pick out the rectangular humps of sod that are slowly softening with age hidden beneath a dense layer of leaves and plant matter.

It's hard to make sense of the building outlines scattered in the forest, but with the use of GPS plotting a map has been created that reveals the formalized institutional distribution of structures around the old parade square. It's impressive. At its zenith, the site covered more than three hundred acres. Unravelling the mysteries of a site so large seems a daunting challenge to me.

Sadly, Ms. Castillo showed me an area where vandals had recently disturbed the site. She lamented how this thoughtless act disrupts the historical context. The stolen artifact is usually placed on someone's mantelpiece where most of its true meaning is lost and forgotten. Everyone is a loser, I realized, even the vandals.

Ms. Castillo told me that the real value of archeological sites is found in the context that is created when information is carefully recorded during excavation. Everything is plotted before removal, then bagged, analyzed and stored with care so that future generations may enjoy and learn from what is being uncovered.

We returned to the shelter of the canopy where Grant had laid out some of the artifacts recovered from their test excavations. We looked through some fascinating bits and pieces of the past. An old shell casing (45–75 WCF) may have been used in the standard-issue Model 1876 Winchester rifle that was supplied by the Mounted Police at the time. Fragments of ceramic, butchered bone and the sole of a tiny shoe are also among the treasures. We debated whether the sole was the remaining bit of a child's shoe or woman's. Amidst the other specimens we examined was a section of heavy twisted wire. Something in its pattern captured my interest. As I turned it over the significance became obvious: it made up the letters MP. I conjured up an image of one of the officers fashioning this simple sign reading NWMP to add distinction to their newly constructed post.

As they continue to gather information, Ms. Castillo and her team will assemble a clearer picture of Tagish Post, of what was here and what went on so many years ago. It will be a fascinating story for all of us to enjoy.

The House that Gold Built

I was the team leader in the restoration of the Commissioner's Residence in Dawson City. This work extended over eight years and involved the participation of as many as two hundred people. By the time the project was finished, I felt like I knew the history of every nail and artifact that went into the building. Completion of this project came at a time of trying personal circumstances for me, and having something to distract me was a blessing. This was one of the most challenging and satisfying projects of my thirty-one-year career at Parks Canada . . .

You may think of the classic Yukon building as a tiny log cabin, overlooking a small lake or river in a hidden corner of the territory. But the gold rush spawned a burst of construction that included some very elegant turn-of-the-century homes. The most elaborate of that era, and of perhaps even today, is the Commissioner's Residence in Dawson City.

The building has a colourful past. It originally served the same function as the White House in Washington, DC—that of housing the top honcho in the territorial government. That person was, at the time, the commissioner of the Yukon. The house was built on a base of gold, the metal that ignited the overnight colonization of the Yukon and sparked the Klondike stampede. At one time it was even painted a muted shade of gold, as it is again today.

The most famous residents were the Blacks, George and Martha to be

The Commissioner's Residence, now restored, must have been an impressive sight on the Dawson waterfront in the years after the gold rush. MICHAEL GATES

exact, who became a political powerhouse in Yukon politics during the first half of the twentieth century.

Once the Klondike was proven to be a substantial find, rather than a flash-in-the-pan phenomenon, the federal government realized that they would have to invest in permanent infrastructure. The Department of Public Works sent an architect by the name of Thomas W. Fuller to construct a post office, courthouse, school, telegraph office, an administration building, and a residence for its most prominent civil servant.

The building, completed in 1901, started its life as a box-shaped structure in the government reserve, in the middle of a mucky and unfinished lot on Front Street, overlooking the mighty Yukon River. It was transformed during the era of Commissioner Congdon into a gingerbread wonder with elaborate verandas and little cupolas on the front façade that cynical citizens called "ballot boxes" because of the corrupt electoral practices associated with the Congdon regime. The building was gutted by fire on the Christmas Eve of 1905. Some years later, it was renovated to the configuration that we

The study in the Commissioner's Residence looked like this when George Black lived here from 1912 to 1916. MICHAEL GATES

see today. The four-year tenure of Commissioner George Black and his wife Martha was terminated in 1916 by World War I and the building stood un-occupied until 1950. When the hospital at the north end of town burned down, the Sisters of St. Ann convinced the federal government to let them use it to house indigent elderly men. Fifteen years later, the Sisters shut the facility down, and the building came into the possession of Parks Canada after it was recognized as being of national significance by the Historic Sites and Monuments Board of Canada.

As part of Parks Canada's contribution to the celebration of the gold-rush centennials, a plan was conceived to restore the building to its historical appearance during the residency of George and Martha Black (1912–1916). Despite the eclectic mix of government purchases that furnished the resi-dence during the post-fire era, George and Martha made their mark on the character of the building. Martha made occasional purchases of furnishings, and around 1914 a new sunroom mysteriously appeared at the rear of the second floor. Influenced by the Arts and Crafts movement of the early twen-tieth century, the interior was also personalized by Martha's love of horticul-ture and George's skill as an amateur taxidermist.

Fortunately, when the plan to restore the building and refurnish the main floor was approved in 1988, there was good evidence in photographs and government files to enable an accurate restoration. About seventy per-cent of the original furnishings had survived in a government warehouse in Whitehorse. The project eventually required the involvement of two hun-dred craftspeople and technical specialists from all over the Parks Canada system. Restoration architects and engineers, curators, archeologists, crafts-people, planners and conservators all played a role. Dawson craftsmen Ben Johnson, Paul Blanchard and Brian Reeves reproduced some of the pieces of furniture that had not survived. Luigi Delgrande, a skilled furniture spe-cialist in the conservation workshop in Parks Canada's Ottawa headquarters, took on some of the upholstered furnishings from the fancy drawing room as his final major project before retiring.

Curators from all over the Parks Canada network tracked down other furnishings and arranged for reproductions when originals were no longer available. This work took them far and wide: some of the carpets were repro-duced in Thailand, the only place where the old-fashioned looms survived.

Copies of portraits of the king and queen were obtained from the royal collection in Great Britain.

Local citizens assisted in the project with particular interest and pride. Pieces of furniture that had ended up in private hands were generously returned. In one case, a music cabinet was returned minus its long delicate legs, and furniture conservators in Winnipeg were able to make it as good as new. Photographs and small surviving samples of the original wallpapers were used as examples to commission the fabrication of replicas that matched the original designs. The staff at historic Fort Steele in BC silkscreened one pattern for us when we couldn't find a suitable selection on today's market.

Among the numerous challenges were the many decisions that had to be made to retain the historic fabric and appearance. A sprinkler system to protect the building was designed to minimize its visual impact. New electrical work had to be installed so it would not damage the original fabric. The original light fixtures were rewired to meet modern safety standards, and missing fixtures were replicated in the United States. The original parquet floor on the main level had been severely damaged in the flood of 1979. The construction crew devised ingenious ways to flatten and reinstall the thousands of warped oak tiles. By opening day, the intricate patterns lay flat and shone with a brilliance that hadn't been seen since the floors were originally installed ninety years earlier.

The maintenance crew fussed over the care of the historically accurate species of plants in the flowerbeds, many of which had been grown and planted by Grant Dowdell, a local horticulturist. As the grand opening approached, the staff took special care to protect the flowers from the threat of any early frost.

The efforts of so many hearts, hands and minds paid off. On August 16, 1996, the entire community and every visitor in town showed up to witness Prime Minister Jean Chrétien officially open the building to the public.

Every summer, Parks Canada provides guided tours of this grand building. When you next visit Dawson City, be sure to take advantage of this rich experience. And while doing so, remember that this is not only a historically accurate rendering of a magnificent building, but also the culmination of the efforts of so many people who joined hands and worked together to make the restoration of this Yukon treasure possible.

How the Mounties Got Their Man

Three men set out for a Yukon Christmas dinner and were never seen again. What followed was one of the first examples of the application of forensic crime-scene analysis to convict a ruthless killer. This is the story of the O'Brien murders . . .

It was Christmas day in 1899 when three men left the tiny log roadhouse at Minto on the Yukon River, destined for the Mounted Police station at Hootchikoo where they were to join Corporal Patrick Ryan for roast turkey. They never arrived, and what ensued is a tale of murder and horror that stands out in the annals of Yukon crime.

It all started when Fred Clayson, riding his bicycle and accompanied on foot by Lynn Relfe, left Dawson City a few days earlier to visit family and friends Outside. Slowly working their way up the frozen surface of the Yukon River, they arrived at Minto on Christmas Eve. There they met telegraph-lineman Lawrence Olsen, who had been working in the vicinity and who invited the two travellers to join him at Corporal Ryan's North-West Mounted Police post for Christmas dinner. When the trio left the roadhouse Christmas morning, it was the last time anyone except the killers saw them alive.

A few kilometres up the Yukon from Minto, George O'Brien and another man ironically named Graves lay in wait. As the three travellers passed

The O'Brien murder trial filled the courthouse to overflowing. YUKON ARCHIVES, NATIONAL ARCHIVES OF CANADA, PHOTO 000512

the lookout the two murderers had fashioned earlier, they were shot from ambush. As Olsen and his companions lay in the snow mortally wounded, they were put to death by gunshots to the head. Their belongings were stripped from them and their bodies shoved into the Yukon River through a hole that had been chopped in the ice. After the valuables had been removed, the victims' clothing was burned. Unwanted items were scattered in the snow to be quickly buried by drifts. Graves was never seen again. It is believed O'Brien killed him as well.

In those days, things happened more slowly than they do now. Days passed before the disappearance became a concern. Meanwhile, O'Brien was slowly making his way up the Yukon River. At Tagish, he was arrested on charges pertaining to the theft of goods from caches. Slowly, suspicions turned into the realization that a terrible crime had been committed. Telegrams wired back and forth between various Mounted Police posts communicated the facts as they emerged.

Will Clayson, Fred's brother, was so concerned that he hired a detective

Illustrator Arthur Buel depicted the O'Brien murder trial for readers on the pages of the *Daily Klondike Nugget* newspaper in August of 1901: From top to bottom, George O'Brien and George West, the three victims leaving Minto on Christmas day and a recreation of the murder scene. *DAILY KLONDIKE NUGGET*

to look into the disappearance. Philip Ralph Maguire was powerfully built, with a bushy black moustache and the dogged determination to locate the missing man. Upon reaching the Yukon, the American Maguire teamed up with North-West Mounted Police Constable Alexander Pennycuick, an Englishman, to find evidence of Clayson's whereabouts.

Here is where the story becomes interesting. In the manner of modern-day forensic science, the two men embarked on a quest for clues to the fate of the missing brother. Together, they returned to the vicinity of where the group was headed, and to where O'Brien was seen at about the same time. Locating O'Brien's camp, the two detectives found the remains of a fire. In the ashes they uncovered the remnants of burnt clothing. This was not a damning fact in itself, but who would want to burn clothing in a land where the temperature was reaching forty below?

Carefully, the men inspected the trail that ran through the bush beside the Yukon River. With the meticulous patience of present-day archeologists, they carefully sifted through metre upon metre of winter snow, until they found a frozen pool of blood buried in the drifts where the trail led down to the river. As their search continued they found more frozen pools of blood and then other items that linked these remains to the missing trio. They found receipts in Olsen's name, a fragment of tooth that later matched the dentition of the bullet-shattered jaw of Relfe when his body was finally recovered and keys that opened drawers in a safe in the office of the Clayson family business in Skagway.

Several rifle shell casings were located near the other items buried in the snow. The casings were of the same calibre as the rifle found in O'Brien's nearby camp. The detectives were able to match the nicks found in the blade of an axe that belonged to O'Brien with the marks on trees that had been chopped down to create the lookout that O'Brien and Graves used to secretly watch passersby on the Yukon River ice trail.

For six weeks, the evidence hidden in the snows along the banks of the Yukon River was carefully gathered, inventoried, mapped and measured. When the bodies of the three men were finally recovered from the icy Yukon, revealing the brutal and unnatural nature of their deaths, there was enough evidence to link O'Brien to the crime. In June 1900, O'Brien was charged with the murder of Lynn Relfe. All this time he had been languishing in jail, first in Tagish and then later in Dawson City.

O'Brien's trial took place in July of the following year. It was, in its era, a high-profile event. The courtroom was packed. Crowds of the curious milled around outside the old log courthouse in Dawson City peering in through the windows to catch a glimpse of O'Brien and the proceedings. The events of the trial and the verdict made the newspapers across the country.

The crown had assembled an impressive array of evidence and the testimony of sixty-three witnesses, each of whom contributed a tiny piece to the puzzle that became a highly incriminating set of circumstances. Witnesses could place O'Brien at the scene of the crime at the time of the disappearance of the men. Others connected the possession of certain objects found at the murder site to the three victims. At the time of his arrest, O'Brien even had in his possession items that belonged to the murder victims.

Two witnesses, one of them the notorious felon "Kid" West, described O'Brien's invitation to join him in his murder and robbery scheme. In the end, even the scathing attack by O'Brien's lawyer, Henry Bleeker, on the veracity of West's testimony, could not sway the jury. After less than two hours of deliberation, the jurors returned a verdict of guilty. He was sentenced by the judge to be hanged.

On the morning of August 23, 1901, George O'Brien rose and had a light breakfast. He offered no resistance when officials, the only people in attendance, led him to the scaffold. Unrepentant to the end, O'Brien cursed those present and spewed out a string of accusations against them. Given a final opportunity to confess his guilt, O'Brien refused, maintaining his innocence to the end. At 7:35 a.m., before a small and silent crowd, a newspaper noted that he was "launched into eternity."

Early Gold Mining in the Yukon was a Steamy Affair

When I first came to work as curator in Dawson City, I got into the practice of driving out into the goldfields and exploring the many back roads and trails. In this way, I discovered the profusion of abandoned mining equipment lying about and became aware of the importance of early steam technology. If you are confused by any of the terms used here, I suggest you read my companion article "The Secret Language of Gold," found later in this volume.

If you drive out to the Klondike goldfields and turn up any side road you will eventually find the telltale signs of century-old mining. The first indication is usually the remains of an old cabin or other structure. There were plenty of them because each placer mining claim is only 150 metres long.

Scan the dense overgrowth that has recaptured many of these long-abandoned places and you will find the scattered rusting shells of old steam boilers and the bulky iron corpses of long-forgotten steam engines, pumps and hoists. There used to be more sites scattered about, but time and the resurgence of mining over the past three decades have taken their toll on the old remains. Even so, they still have a story to tell.

The earliest mining in the Yukon was hand-powered. The traditional method of prospecting was a matter of scrambling over mountainous terrain picking up specimens from exposed outcrops, or panning the gravelly bottoms of thousands of tiny streams. The pick and shovel were the basic tools of the trade. If a promising claim was staked, the necessary equipment would be fashioned from locally sawn wood with a small inventory of hand tools. Flumes, sluice boxes and rockers could be quickly and simply assembled to facilitate the extraction of free gold from the frozen ground.

Within a few years of the arrival of the first prospectors, they had perfected the technique of winter drift mining. This was a great advantage because this made it possible to extend their mining from a few warm summer months to a year-round enterprise. No longer did they have to lay idle in their crude log cabins during the long, dark, cold winter months suffering from boredom and cabin fever.

Drift mining was the process of sinking a vertical shaft into the unconsolidated though frozen gravels of the valley bottoms until solid bedrock was reached. At that point, the miner changed direction and tunnelled, or drifted, horizontally along the bedrock across the width of the valley bottom. With any luck the pay streak, gravel peppered with a rich concentration of gold, would be found. This was, and still is, the prospector's fantasy. The paydirt was then hoisted to the surface by hand, using a crudely fashioned windlass.

Drift mining was gruelling, exhausting work and had little chance of success. In the Yukon, miners had to deal with permafrost, which converted the loose, unconsolidated gravels into a compact, solid mass, hard as granite. Working the frozen gravel had both advantages and disadvantages. Permafrost made it possible to excavate underground tunnels without requiring timber cribbing to prevent a collapse. The icy matrix was as hard as rock as long as it remained frozen. The disadvantage was that paydirt had to be thawed in order to remove it from the drift and hoist it to the surface. To thaw the ground properly required skill at preparing and setting carefully controlled fires that would concentrate the heat on the frozen gravel without softening the surrounding excavation and causing it to cave in.

Once the fire was set, the miner got out of the excavation quickly until the fire died down and the tunnel cleared of smoke and deadly fumes. In the old days, this method of mining was slow, dirty, arduous work. Once the riches of the Klondike were realized, miners started importing steam boilers

Hundreds of old boilers like this one lie about the fields of the Klondike, a testimony to the importance of steam in the early days of gold mining. MICHAEL GATES

and steam-powered machinery. These devices reduced the amount of hand labour necessary to get the gold from the ground. Steam-powered pumps removed water accumulating in the mine shafts or elevated it for sluicing. Steam engines powered saws to cut wood to feed the boilers and run windlasses of varying complexity that hoisted and moved gravel from one place to another. Steam reduced the amount of costly manual labour, thus boosting the profitability of a given mining claim.

Gold was discovered in the Klondike in 1896. By 1899, miners on all the creeks were importing steam devices of all shapes and sizes from sophisticated elevating bucket systems and steam shovels to simple hoists. The innovation of a self-tripping bucket, known as a self-dumper, became the most popular tool of the miners. The steam-powered self-dumper was able to lift large buckets of pay gravel from a shaft or open pit, move it to where the paydirt was being stored for sluicing, then dump it in the pile, all untouched by human hands.

Steam could also be used to heat buildings and generate electricity, but perhaps its most unique application in those early days was for thawing frozen ground. This innovation came about, so the story goes, when in the early days of the gold rush claim-holder Clarence Berry on Claim Number 6, Eldorado Creek, noticed that escaping steam was thawing a pile of frozen gravel. Improvising, he connected a steam hose to a gun barrel and shoved it into the frozen pile. The steam worked its miracle and thawed the heap, and so was born the steam thawing point. In no time at all, everyone had replaced the open fire with rows of custom-built steam thawing points to soften the permafrost for excavation.

When dredges came into common use in the goldfields, entire sections of valley bottom in front of them were punctured by hundreds of steam points, all thawing the ground through which they were to pass. On this scale, a company would require thousands of cords of wood every year to feed the hungry boilers that produced the steam. Steam powered just about everything in the Yukon until the internal combustion engine came into common use.

Then being seen as heavy and obsolete, hundreds of steam engines, pumps and hoists, some crudely fashioned, others massive engineering feats, were abandoned in the hills and valleys over hundreds of square kilometres.

The boilers came from as far away as Ohio, New York, Pennsylvania and Victoria, BC. Others were made locally. All testify to the optimism and industry that followed the Klondike gold rush. Although lying abandoned on every creek and pup, they still speak to the hopes and dreams of the men who toiled for fortune a century ago.

Smells Like Gold Rush Spirit

Sometimes a conversation with someone will lead you off in directions you hadn't planned on. That's what happened with this article . . .

I blame this one on Patrick Singh, Whitehorse musician and entrepreneur, who talked to me about the history of music in the territory. For some reason, this triggered a train of thought about the sounds and smells of the gold rush. Remember, the gold rush belonged to a time before computers, Internet, iPods, MP3 players, CDs, LPs, TV and radio. Telephones connected by wires were state-of-the-art technology back then. Young readers will have a hard time imagining this world because it isn't even described in textbooks. For some, a world without a computer is almost inconceivable.

The truth is our spirit has never been restrained by a lack of technology. Before modern advances, the human race found many ways to create entertainment and add pleasure to daily routines. So why don't we take a sensory journey into the past, with a walk through Dawson City during the gold rush.

". . . We came to a place where there was a sign that read 'The Sky is the Limit,'" wrote one new arrival in the Klondike, ". . . Incessant music greeted our ears . . . caused by a piano thumper who played on an old loose-keyed piano which obviously had seen better days. Baritone and bass voices burst into snatches of unsteady song as the musician improvised from one familiar tune to another. At intervals a tired-faced violinist played on a melancholy, whiny-sounding violin."

From the swamp behind Sam Bonnifield's Bank Saloon came the sounds of a wheezy portable organ and the tap of dancing feet. The heavenly voices of the Oatley Sisters belted out such tunes as "Break the News to Mother" and "She's Only a Bird in a Gilded Cage" to tearful homesick miners. Another young singer whose voice dampened the eyes of grown men far from home was nine-year-old Margie Newman, whom they showered with gold nuggets when she performed on stage at the Tivoli Theatre.

Curiously, decades after the gold rush, people remembered songs being performed in Dawson City that weren't written until many years after the great stampede. In the 1950s, in the name of tourism, the cancan dance, of which there was absolutely no sign during the gold rush, was introduced into popular mythology. What the gold-rush miners had longed for were songs that reminded them of their faraway homes, and entertainment that masked the fact that they were living in a harsh wilderness rather than in Paris, London or New York. The saloons, gaming houses and dance halls, crammed together along Front Street, reeked of liquor, tobacco and sweat, and emitted the sounds of ratcheting gaming wheels, shuffled cards, clattering chips, raucous laughter, dancing and tinkling keyboards.

Crowds roared at the boxing matches that were popular events at the time. Along the Front Street of 1898, everything was in Technicolor, not the black and white of the faded old photographs of the era. No car engine or boat motor intruded into the auditory landscape. No automobile exhaust assaulted the nose back then. Steam was the order of the day, a much quieter form of power than those we are now familiar with. Yet even steam brought with it the crashing of cordwood and the slamming of firebox doors on dozens of steamers.

In the crowds that moved along the riverfront, we might have heard throngs of heavy boots trampling the boardwalk or hundreds of voices merged in countless conversations in many different languages though English was predominant. Men would be advertising their wares in loud voices from their storefronts. Flags flapped in the wind. Every special event held during the summer was accompanied by the sounds of hastily assembled brass bands and shouts from the crowds. The celebration of the Fourth of

In 1898, Dawson City was an exotic, crowded place, filled with strange sights, sounds and smells. YUKON ARCHIVES, VANCOUVER PUBLIC LIBRARY FONDS, PHOTO #02095

July was accompanied by thunderous salutes of gunfire that terrified every dog in town. It was days before many of the frightened canines returned to their masters.

We would have heard horses, the clatter of wagons and commotion of freight being loaded and unloaded. Before the streets were well established, they turned into mudholes after every rainstorm. Wagons were mired down to their axles, and I can clearly imagine the curses of the teamsters as they attempted to extricate the loads and struggling beasts from their mucky confinement.

During the summer, the air would have been filled with a chorus of howls from the countless sled dogs, tethered, underfed and bored. To avoid the strictures about business on the Sabbath, entrepreneurs chartered paddlewheel steamers, stuffed them with gamblers and high-lifes, and churned downriver to Alaska. When the boats finally limped back to Dawson's dock days later, they were cheered by thousands of onlookers, combined with the blasting of the steamers' whistles and howling of dogs.

The racket of chopping, sawing and hammering would have assailed us from every direction as hundreds of buildings were rapidly assembled in the scramble to cash in on business opportunities and meet the demand for homes. The clatter was magnified by the flurry of activity at the government woodpile, where those convicted of petty crimes fulfilled their sentences by cutting wood. Doors of the blacksmith shops would have opened onto the avenues behind Front Street, and the clanging of hammer upon steel and whoosh of the forge would have flooded out into the street. Farther down the avenue, the linotypes of the first newspapers would have been chattering away as the type fell into place and the presses turned.

Sawmills were operating around the clock, with saw blades whining and protesting under the strain. Intermingled with the scent of newly cut timber and the fresh smells of nature would be the heavy aroma of thousands of unwashed bodies, horse sweat and manure. There was no sewage disposal at the height of the gold rush, no sanitation or advances in medicine. Dawson became a fetid pool of filth that cultured diseases along with a stench that filled the atmosphere. The typhoid epidemic that resulted packed the hospital and kept the martyred Father William Judge caring for the sick around the clock. The air was thick with the pall of woodsmoke from forest fires and the chimneys of thousands of stoves.

It was a carnival-like atmosphere that permeated Dawson City for a brief exciting year during the gold rush. Close your eyes and give reign to your imagination. Conjure up the sights, sounds and smells of the era. Marvel at how exciting a time it was and how this sensory overload enhanced the feeling that something extraordinary was taking place.

THE DALTON TRAIL

Jack Dalton and the Shooting of Dan McGinnis

Jack Dalton and the Dalton Trail are an intriguing but little-known aspect of Yukon history. I first became ensnared by this topic in 1972 when I was appalled by a wanton disregard for the historic fabric of the Yukon displayed by a local miner who bulldozed several of the buildings at Dalton Post. I campaigned to have Dalton Post and the adjacent village of Neskatahéen declared nationally significant . . . and failed. However, this process gave me enough of a connection with the people and the place that I wanted to learn more and also correct some of the misinformation commonly believed about the man and the trail.

The Dalton Trail starts near Haines, Alaska, on the Pacific coast, ascending the coastal range to the interior over the Chilkat Pass along a route now followed by the Haines Highway. It veers north from the highway at Klukshu, then along the east side of Dezadeash Lake. It crosses the Alaska Highway at Champagne, continuing north to the Hutchi Lakes, then follows the Nordenskjold River to the present-day town of Carmacks. From there, the trail parallels the Yukon along both banks to sites below the Five Finger and Rink Rapids. On the east side of the river, it continues to a point opposite Fort Selkirk.

As I discuss earlier in this book, the trail was not discovered by Dalton. It was used by First Nations long before Dalton arrived in the area, and "Dalton Trail" was a term bestowed upon the route by the newspapers of the time.

"**Y**ou're a dirty, lying sonofabitch. You take it back!" growled Jack Dalton, and with that, he drew his gun and put six slugs into Jack McGinnis right there in the saloon.

This is the contemporary portrayal of Jack Dalton shooting Dan McGinnis in 1893. McGinnis was thought to be a blowhard and ne'er-do-well who had it coming when Dalton pumped him full of lead. Several accounts have McGinnis spreading a rumour that Dalton had a sloop full of illicit whiskey anchored off Skagway (or Haines—take your pick) that he was going to sell to the Natives, and Dalton was not about to have his reputation ruined. Dalton immediately turned himself in and was quickly exonerated by his peers. Sound like a tale out of the Wild West with a good guy, bad guy, tarnished reputations and guns blazing in the local saloon?

This portrayal, which is typical of many recent accounts of the shooting, was inspired by an earlier book by Martha McKeown called *The Trail Led North*. Published in 1948, McKeown's book is based on a narrative of her uncle Mont Hawthorn who was in Alaska before the great gold rush. "For many months we have worked together," said McKeown at the time she wrote down Hawthorn's narrative, "getting things down straight. He has insisted on accuracy in every detail. Everything in this book has been told exactly as it happened, set down in his own words."

So it must be true, right? Over the ensuing years, many authors have borrowed and modified elements of this colourful narrative to retell the story. The truth is it didn't happen that way. Dalton's altercation with McGinnis didn't occur in Skagway, as reported by one writer, and it didn't take place in a saloon. McGinnis didn't get six slugs in the chest and his name wasn't even Jack. It was Dan. The original transcripts and documents from the trial of Jack Dalton for the murder of Daniel McGinnis are housed in the United States National Archives and they paint a very different picture. According to the sworn testimony of the main eyewitness, Patrick Woods, on March 6, 1893, Dalton walked into Murray's Cannery store in Haines where the sixty-eight-kilogram McGinnis worked as a clerk, and accused him of telling lies. Apparently, McGinnis had told members of the Chilkat Tlingit that Dalton was going to develop a trail and set up a trading business in the southwest Yukon. The Chilkat had up to that time held a trade monopoly in the area. Forty years earlier, the Chilkat had travelled hundreds of kilometres into the Yukon to burn down the trading post of the mighty Hudson's Bay Company in order to retain control of local trade.

Dalton grabbed the surprised clerk, pulled out a pistol, and started hitting the seated McGinnis over the head with the butt, repeating "you're a liar!" with each blow. The fourth blow caused the gun to go off, wounding McGinnis in the shoulder. Dalton swung one more time, punching the injured man in the stomach, and discharging a fatal bullet into his gut. McGinnis was brought to Juneau for medical care but didn't live long enough for the doctor to treat him. A warrant for Dalton's arrest was issued the following day and an officer was sent to Haines to bring him back to Juneau for the trial that took place in late June.

The court hearing was short, and relied heavily on Woods' sworn testimony. When the jury brought back a not-guilty verdict, the response, according to the press of the day, was extremely divided. One newspaper reported the people in the gallery cheered upon hearing the verdict, while another

Jack Dalton was a remarkable outdoorsman and entrepreneur with a fiery temper. MACBRIDE MUSEUM OF YUKON HISTORY, ACC #1989-1-1-220

stated there was much outrage over the decision. The *Sitka Alaskan* claimed that an angry mob intent on lynching Dalton was finally convinced to give him three days to get out of town. The members of the jury, working for the big mine in Juneau, were all fired and reportedly left town shortly after.

And what about the lies that Dalton accused McGinnis of telling? Well, they weren't lies after all. Dalton went on to develop the original Native travel routes to the Yukon into a corridor called the Dalton Trail for transporting livestock to Dawson City during the gold rush. The Chilkat tried to sabotage his enterprise and even attempted to kill him several times without success. Dalton went on to a variety of other successful business ventures over the years, and as his fortunes improved so did his reputation. In later years, he had many influential friends and contacts.

So what was Dalton really like? His exploits in the wilds of the Yukon and Alaska are legendary. He was an excellent horseman, a good cook, and he had a compass hard-wired into his brain. It was said that if he ever went over a piece of country, he never forgot it. Edward Glave, the English explorer who travelled into the Yukon with Dalton on two separate expeditions, called him the best all-round man he ever knew. Given the circumstances, this is strong praise for the hardy pioneer entrepreneur.

Dalton also had another reputation: that of a tough, almost menacing figure. Author Edward Morgan described him this way: ". . . a diminutive figure with broad and powerful shoulders somewhat out of proportion to his stature. He was always pre-eminently fit and in condition as he would need to be to perform on the trail as he did. He was an agreeable man and square shooting person to do business with, but a bad hombre to cross or run up against."

Crossing Dalton was a risky decision to make. He was alleged to have killed Matt Egan in Oregon when confronted after he fired the man. He also beat to a pulp a man from Haines named Tim Vogel for supplying his workmen with liquor. He is reputed to have followed a party who refused to pay a toll for using his route for herding cattle to the Klondike, threatening to kill them if they ever set foot on his trail again. In later years, he punched out a government agent in Cordova when the man held back on the approval of Dalton's payroll money on a contract. When his business interests were threatened, he occasionally used force to get his way.

Dalton was small in size, but left a giant imprint in the pioneer history of Yukon and Alaska. His true-life exploits earned him a legendary reputation. It clearly wasn't necessary to fabricate a Hollywood-style gunfight to achieve it.

Escape from Famine

When I wrote this, it was the winter of 2008–09. I had been watching the news with interest. The price of food was rising rapidly and the economy was in free-fall, and there was debate over the cause; some argued that the rising demand for oil was at the centre of the problem, while others argued that they are two independent issues, and that oil and food did not mix. Naturally, I turned to the historical accounts to get a perspective on the food situation . . .

In the fall of 1897, there was a food shortage in the bustling new gold-rush centre of Dawson City. Barely a year old, Dawson was attracting thousands of people from all over the world; people eager to get there and get rich, regardless of the risk. But the north was an isolated and remote place, unable to accommodate the requirements of the growing hoard.

Many who came did not bring enough food. In Dawson City, the merchants were eyeing the diminishing supply with growing unease. Where were the steamers with the winter provisions? Several ships were supposedly on their way. Captain J.E. Hansen of the Alaska Commercial Company, one of the community's most important suppliers, set off downstream to investigate. He found the steamers hopelessly marooned by low water at Fort Yukon, over four hundred kilometres downriver from Dawson.

Knowing that food was not coming, he struggled back upstream to

Dawson against a strong current in an ice-clogged Yukon River to pass on the message. "Men of Yukon!" he announced, "There will be no boats until spring. I advise all who are out of provisions or who don't have enough to carry you through the winter to make a dash for the Outside. There is no time to lose!"

Prices went through the roof. Flour that sold for one dollar a sack Outside was two dollars a pound in Dawson that fall. Steaks that sold elsewhere for a few cents a pound were selling for two and a half dollars. Everyone was jealously hoarding their food supply. The Mounted Police instituted a policy that those coming into the Yukon must bring enough supplies with them to last a year. This amounted to five hundred kilograms of goods for every person entering the territory.

However, this new mandate did nothing to address the immediate problem. What followed was a wild exodus from the gold-rush town. The steamer *Bella* was chartered by the Mounted Police and two hundred men were reported to have accepted free passage downriver, comfortable in the knowledge that if they made it as far as Fort Yukon or Circle City they would find stranded steamers with ample food to carry them through the winter.

Others wanted more than an escape from starvation; some wanted to get back to their families; others were seeking investors for their mining ventures. For them, the only choice was to head upriver with hope of making it to the coast via the Dalton Trail.

On October 14, the Thomas McGee party of four miners left Dawson City for Fort Selkirk poling upstream in a canoe. Four days out they encountered serious obstacles in crossing a few hundred metres of the Yukon River where the water was too deep to use their poles. It took them two hours, during which time they nearly foundered amongst the ice floes. The ice grew worse until the ninth day when they found themselves beached in a slough, with a raging current, high banks and overhanging trees. It seemed as though they could go no further. At this point, however, they had a stroke of good luck. Renowned pathfinder Jack Dalton and an unidentified First Nation companion in a four-metre shell caught up with them. They joined forces, and after four days of struggle arrived at Fort Selkirk. They rested there for two days.

There weren't any supplies at Fort Selkirk either, so despite warnings

In the summer of 1897, Dawson City was rapidly growing and the food supply couldn't keep up. LIBRARY OF CONGRESS, DIGITAL ID PPMSCA 08703

from Dalton of the conditions that lay before them, they forged on with him and five horses following the Yukon riverbank for ninety kilometres. With over twenty centimetres of snow on the ground when they started and more falling daily, things didn't look good for the horses, which had to paw through the snow to get to the grass beneath. They struggled into Carmack's Post through sixty centimetres of snow then turned south and started over Dalton's trail. Six days later, they made it to the Southern Tutchone village of Hutchi.

McGee described the difficult conditions they encountered: "On the summit of the surrounding mountains heavy gales and snow were prevailing. Bad water beyond Hootchy-Eye poisoned most of the party, causing severe and frequent cramps and hemorrhages. We got only two meals a day the entire trip, breakfast always in the dark between 4 and 6, and dinner between 4 and 5."

Six days out of Hutchi, they arrived in Dalton Post, where they had a sumptuous and reviving meal consisting of canned corn beef, canned cold tomatoes and bread baked by Dalton. By the time they had arrived two of the horses had perished. It was remarkable that any survived. Another group coming in from the coast had started out with a dozen animals, and shot the last of them as they arrived at the post. The McGee company plodded on, day after day through snow that had already reached a metre in depth. They finally arrived at Haines after forty-two days of arduous travel.

Another party, consisting of "Klondike" Joe Boyle and "Swiftwater" Bill Gates and a number of others, made it to Haines Mission—but much of the credit for their surviving the trip was given to the heroic efforts of Boyle, who kept them going when they felt like giving up.

Nobody starved in Dawson City that winter, but the early-autumn reports painted a bleak picture. The United States government decided to take action and sponsored a relief expedition to save the starving miners in the Canadian mining town.

Only the threat of starvation and a foolhardy obsession to reach civilization could motivate travellers to risk the hazards of the Chilkat Pass and snowbound Yukon trails in the deepest, coldest part of the winter. I wonder what First Nations observers, living in harmony with the cycle of the seasons, thought of the crazy antics of these white men.

One Woman's Gold Rush

While women made up only a small percentage of the stampede of hopefuls who came to the Klondike during the gold rush, they were nevertheless an important part of the story. I was once told that very little had been documented about their experiences, yet when I sat down with a pen and paper, I was able to fill a page quickly with references to books and articles on the topic. And while women in the Klondike were scarce, there were even fewer who came by way of the Dalton Trail . . .

"Gold! Gold! Gold!"

The front-page headline of the *Seattle Post-Intelligencer* proclaimed a ton of gold arriving in Seattle July 17, 1897. It sparked a stampede unlike anything we will see again: the Klondike Gold Rush!

While the allure of gold in the far north mainly attracted men, women were also influenced by "Klondicitis."

Women were indirectly affected when their sweethearts, husbands, brothers and fathers set off for the Klondike seeking fortune and adventure. But a small percentage of women came north as well. While some, like Della Murray Banks, were well equipped for what was to come, most were ill-prepared for the experience.

In New York, the Women's Klondike Expedition Syndicate was formed by the Big Apple's social cream. The Syndicate made plans for forty members to hire two Pullman sleeping cars to transport them in comfort by rail across the continent, then up the coast by ship to Sitka. At Sitka, they were to travel on by self-contained horse-drawn caravans to Dawson. For each group of twenty women, there would be three vans equipped with sleeping quarters, while two more would carry provisions. There is no record, however, of the expedition ever departing.

The wife of Senator Stewart of Nevada was also stricken with a bad case of Klondike fever. Mrs. Stewart announced she was going to follow her oldest grandson on the trail to Dawson City. As a young bride she had lived the hard life on the frontier in Virginia City, and now a grandmother she was determined to seek adventure again.

In Seattle, three women announced they were incorporating the Women's Yukon Alaska Mining and Investment Company. They planned to use capital raised to hire men to go to the Klondike and work mining claims for a share of the gold they recovered.

Another scheme, The Women's Clondyke Expedition, took five hundred women by boat around the southern tip of South America on their way to Skagway. They were shipwrecked in the Straits of Magellan, and when they finally reached Seattle, threw in the towel and headed home.

The relatively small number of women who did make it to the Klondike had their eyes opened. Some thought they could get over the Klondike trails without spoiling their appearance, soiling their clothes, or letting a hair fall out of place. In reality, they faced hundreds of kilometres of exhausting travel, sickness, starvation, severe cold, avalanches, storms and dangerous rapids.

Two women actually travelled with a circus-like entourage that included a portable bowling alley. Another was seen on the Dalton Trail wearing farmer's overalls and a fancy hat, and carrying a canary in a cage as a precaution against mine gas!

Yet another woman set out with a syndicate of stampeders from the eastern United States. She was the only female among one hundred men destined to reach the Klondike by crossing the glacier-covered coastal mountains from Yakutat Bay. "... The journey is only 425 miles," proclaimed one Alaskan newspaper of this route, "and that ... over rolling grassland! No mountains to ascend, no passes to plod through, probably no deep mud fields to wade across, and, most certainly, no great extremes of cold to endure." This was one of the most tragic attempts of all; forty of the hundred perished on the Malaspina and Nunatak glaciers. The rest survived starvation, scurvy and snow blindness, but never reached the Klondike. For the sole woman in the group, the expedition must have been hell, and there is no record of whether or not she was one of the survivors.

One hardy spirit who travelled over the Dalton Trail in 1898 was Della Murray Banks. Accompanying her husband Austin and a party of nine others in search of gold, she was no newcomer to northern conditions, having made three previous trips to Alaska. During an earlier excursion she had burned her hand and lost two fingers, and had proved she could adjust herself to

Della Murray Banks on her horse Polly. She started out with a blanket to sit on and a rope for a halter. It wasn't long before she had a fine saddle and bridle, picked up from along the trail. DELLA MURRAY BANKS PHOTO, *ALASKA SPORTSMAN*

any situation, an admirable trait for anyone journeying to the Klondike. In her account of the Dalton Trail voyage, published in the *Alaska Sportsman* in 1945, Mrs. Banks wryly commented on some of the men in her party: "It wasn't the man who didn't know, but the man who wouldn't learn, that made it hard."

She was assigned a durable, steady pack horse named Polly as a mount, and rode her with only a blanket and rope surcingle. Polly had not stirrups,

Della Murray Banks made ninety biscuits every day regardless of the weather or conditions on the trail. DELLA MURRAY BANKS PHOTO, *ALASKA SPORTSMAN*

Apron over boots and men's pants were standard issue for Della Murray Banks' trip over the Dalton Trail. DELLA MURRAY BANKS PHOTO, *ALASKA SPORTSMAN*

nor saddle or bridle, just a rope halter for guidance. Fortunately, the horse simply followed the trail at a slow and steady pace.

Mrs. Banks was hired on at fifty dollars a month to cook for the party. Every day, regardless of location or weather, she prepared meals for the ten hungry men using a flimsy sheet-metal stove under the open sky. Each evening, she baked ninety biscuits, fifteen at a time, more often than not on her knees in order to access her work surface. At the end of one hard day, one of the party suggested to her that if it were up to him to make supper there would have been no meal prepared that night. In response to this remark, she simply observed that she had walked the same distance that he had, and had prepared the evening meal as usual!

At Pyramid Harbor, the starting point of the journey, Della met two other ladies who were to accompany the group. One regarded the trip as a lark, wanting to go just for the fun of it, and didn't expect to do any work. She claimed she wouldn't think of going if there was any possibility of getting her feet wet! She couldn't ride a horse—and at best it would be a three-hundred mile trip. She refused to drink or eat from a tin cup or plate, and would not consider a meal of beans or bacon, preferring cream, milk and eggs. Mrs. Banks declared she wouldn't go if the two women went. "I was willing to do my share," she said, "but that didn't include waiting on Mrs. Tucker." The two ladies finally decided to spend the summer in Seattle, where they could keep their feet dry. Mrs. Banks smiled when she heard that, and said, "They don't know Seattle!"

Nineteenth-century society had not prepared most women for the trials that came with a trip over a Klondike trail. First Nation women, however, were raised in a different culture and lived and travelled in the north with ease and familiarity. When a woman from the city streets of New York, Vancouver or Seattle ventured north the summer of 1898—going against the social grain to do so—it was truly a testimony to her determination and spirit.

The Hellish Reindeer Caper of 1898

The frenzy that resulted when gold-laden ships arrived in Seattle and San Francisco led to some bizarre ventures. The event described here is one of the weirdest of all. Communication was slow in 1897, and conflicting reports were received in Washington regarding the conditions in the Klondike. As well, American legislators were either unaware or unconcerned about the Klondike being in another country. When reading about this undertaking, the word boondoggle came to mind...

"The northern lights have seen queer sights," said Yukon bard Robert Service, and surely one of the queerest had to be the reindeer caper of 1898.

When word of the discovery of gold on the Klondike leaked out of the Yukon in 1897 it set off the stampede to Dawson City. The newspapers were full of articles about impending food shortages in the Klondike. Canadian government officials warned citizens of the risks, yet thousands still embarked on the journey of a lifetime.

The North-West Mounted Police, under the direction of Sam Steele, implemented the one-ton rule, requiring stampeders to bring enough supplies to feed themselves for a year in the north. This undoubtedly saved the hides of many inexperienced gold seekers.

The Lapps used their reindeer to haul supplies through the wilderness route to the starving miners of the Klondike. They were fifteen months late. YUKON ARCHIVES, J.B. TYRRELL PAPERS, THOMAS FISHER RARE BOOK LIBRARY, UNIVERSITY OF TORONTO, 82/15, PHOTO #368

Meanwhile, the Mounted Police in Dawson City were encouraging miners low on provisions to pack and leave before freeze-up. They arranged for two hundred men to travel downriver on the steamer *Bella*; others were making their way upriver and out of the country over the Dalton Trail.

The potential famine in Dawson became a topic of debate in Washington, DC. Possibly unaware of the precise location of the Klondike in Canada, confused by conflicting reports about the food situation in the Klondike and swayed by the vigorous lobbying of Alaska's well-known Presbyterian missionary Sheldon Jackson, the US government approved a bill to provide $200,000 to finance a relief expedition in the form of a herd of reindeer to the Klondike. Whether the animals would carry the much-needed food, or *be* the actual food is not clear.

Jackson immediately set off for Norway, where he secured five hundred and thirty-eight reindeer, fifteen Lapp herdsmen and two hundred and fifty tons of reindeer moss to sustain the animals on the long journey ahead. The herd crossed the Atlantic by steamer. They were then transported by rail to Seattle where they were transferred to a three-masted barque, the *Seminole*, for the trip to Alaska.

Although it was unknown to the expedition, by the time they arrived on the west coast, the need for aid had passed. Meanwhile, this relief expedition was suffering from the same problem that they were intended to solve: starvation. Reindeer require a specialized diet of moss and cannot live on the grasses commonly fed to cattle and other livestock. Four died in Seattle while waiting for transport to Alaska, and another eight expired on the voyage north.

The situation worsened as the herd arrived at Haines Mission (now Haines), Alaska, on March 29, 1898. The reindeer were dropping like flies. The herd was moved inland toward the mountains where there was some moss for grazing but the deep snow in the mountain passes blocked their way to larger supplies farther inland. By the time they were able to move over the mountains on the Dalton Trail in the middle of May, only 164 remained.

All that summer, the reindeer expedition wandered about the southwest Yukon. The food supply for the herders was also limited, so to ensure there would be enough provisions for the remaining herders fifteen of the men were sent back to Haines and then on to Seattle.

By June 23, another eighteen animals had perished. The animals frequently wandered off into the nearby mountains and had to be brought back to the trail. After crossing the summit, they turned west and followed the Alsek River (now the Tatshenshini) for several days before doubling back. They took to the peaks on the east side of the Dalton Trail and by the time they got to the Mendenhall River, they had to send some of their party sixty-five kilometres back to Dalton Post to get more supplies,

The party kept moving through swamps, over mountaintops, through dense brush and across raging streams while suffering from continual attacks from hordes of mosquitoes. By the end of September, they had made it as far as the Southern Tutchone village of Hutchi. From Dalton's crude trading post located there, they were able to obtain additional supplies to last them until the middle of December.

They turned west at Hutchi, crossed the Aishihik River and moved northwest past the Native village of Aishihik and through the Nisling River on their way to the White River. By the middle of October, they were fighting the early-winter snows. They were not prepared for the cold and were running out of supplies for the third time. The reindeer were thin and weak, and there were attacks by wolves. Finally they reached White River and followed it down to the Yukon River. At Stewart Island the group was able to re-provision. Christmas came and went. Eventually, on January 27, 1899, they passed through Dawson. A month later they reached their ultimate destination of Circle, Alaska, with the remaining 114 animals. It is alleged that when they arrived one of the Lapps approached their leader and said: "Do you think there is any hell worse than this one?" "No," he responded, "I think this is all the hell we want."

In Circle City, the reindeer were tended by the US Army, who decided to use the entire herd for transport to the Tanana River. En route, they encountered a herd of caribou, and most of the reindeer joined their wild cousins. The remainder were slaughtered and given to the miners in that vicinity.

Ironically, the relief expedition arrived at its destination almost a year and a half after the food panic, with only a fraction of the herd. In the end, it was the relief expedition that was more in need of relief than the miners of the Klondike.

Cattle Drives to the Yukon

When I started my study of the Dalton Trail, I didn't know that one of its most significant roles was as a route over which thousands of head of livestock were driven to feed the hungry miners at Dawson City during the gold rush . . .

When you think of the great cattle drives of the pioneer west, the famous Chisholm Trail in the United States or the big ranches of Alberta come to mind. But the longest and most challenging trail rides were to the Yukon. The motivation was a quick profit—and the risks were high.

The first cattle drive in the Yukon took place over the Dalton Trail in 1896, before the Klondike gold rush. Willis Thorp, a merchant from Juneau, took a herd of forty cattle over the trail, heading for the town of Forty Mile, the trading centre of the Fortymile and Sixtymile mining areas. The Thorp outfit drove the cattle through four hundred kilometres of wild country to the Yukon River, and then continued along the west bank to a point below the Rink Rapids where the herd was loaded onto rafts to be floated downriver. The herders came upon a scene of frenzied construction at the mouth of the Klondike River where prospectors hearing of the new discovery were flocking by the dozens, so it is not known how much of the herd ever made it to Forty Mile.

For the miners, forced to live on a monotonous diet of wild meat, bacon, beans and biscuits, fresh beef was a big treat. Some of it made it all the way to Alaska, where newspapers reported in March and April of 1897 that: "The first beefsteak that ever reached Circle City sold for forty-eight dollars per pound a few weeks ago. The steaks consisted of a ten-pound piece of beef slaughtered at Forty-Mile Creek, packed and shipped four hundred kilometres to Circle City by Thomas O'Brien. When O'Brien reached camp, the miners turned out in a body to see the steak. It was placed on exhibition and attracted as much attention as an eight-legged calf..."

A price of forty-eight dollars for a steak got the attention of the ranchers on the prairies, where beef was selling for six to nine cents a pound. Prairie ranchers started having dreams that would make Midas blush. For the next few years, cattle from as far away as Oregon, Manitoba and Saskatchewan were transported to the coast by train, loaded onto boats and shipped north

The Dalton Trail was the main route for transporting cattle from the Alaskan coast to Dawson City. YUKON ARCHIVES, J.B. TYRRELL PAPERS, THOMAS FISHER RARE BOOK LIBRARY, UNIVERSITY OF TORONTO, 82/15, PHOTO #6

to Haines and Skagway, then overland to where they could be loaded, dead or alive, onto rafts and barges for the journey down the Yukon to Dawson City.

The distances travelled were greater than those of the Chisholm Trail. The terrain was harsh and unfamiliar, and the risk was high for the cattlemen. They could get lost, and feed could also be a problem—a skinny cow wouldn't bring much profit in Dawson City. Along the trail, livestock were subject to predators, disease, swamps and ever-present mosquitoes. They drowned in raging rivers and were sucked into quicksand. The weather could be hostile, and the seasons worked against them. Woe to the cattleman who started his herd over the trail too late in the summer!

On the Dalton Trail, before reaching Canada, the cattle drivers had to pay a toll to Jack Dalton's men: two dollars and fifty cents per cow and fifty cents per goat, sheep or swine. There were plenty of herders who paid up. During the summers of 1897 and '98, thousands of cattle, horses and sheep travelled to the Yukon over the Dalton Trail.

Each herder came north with dreams of making a big profit in Dawson City, but it was hit and miss. Three who made their way over the Dalton Trail late in the summer of '98 found that out. Arriving in the Yukon, their herds were slaughtered and rafted downstream. Both the slaughtering and raft building were time consuming and labour intensive. With winter closing in, it was a race against time. One herd was butchered and shipped when the weather was too warm: most of the meat spoiled on the voyage downriver. Part of the shipment got stranded on a bar in the Yukon River with the water level falling. The herders had to jettison 128 quarters of beef before they could manhandle their scow back into the ice-filled current.

The next herd, belonging to Pat Burns of Calgary and driven by cattleman Billy Henry, arrived at the Yukon shortly after. The nine men set about constructing corrals, building rafts twenty-two metres by nine metres, and slaughtering one hundred and eighty steers, each weighing seven hundred and thirty kilograms. As the cool October weather enveloped the herders, the carcasses froze to prevent spoilage. In a race against time, the cattlemen steered their ungainly rafts downriver and arrived safely before freeze-up. The North-West Mounted Police purchased seventy-five thousand pounds of that meat at seventy-five cents a pound, while the remainder sold at a dollar a pound, yielding a small fortune for the summer's labour. Other cattlemen travelling a few days behind Billy Henry weren't so fortunate; they either received a lower price for their meat, or the river froze before they could bring their product downstream.

The waste left behind at Yukon Crossing proved to be a valuable commodity. Three mushers passing along the trail saw an opportunity, spent the winter serving up the offal from the butchering to passing teams for dog feed, and made a dollar a pound for their effort.

Other herds were driven over the White Pass and floated downriver, braving treacherous rapids along the way, as well as the tempestuous waters of Lake Laberge. One was brought up over the Telegraph Trail, championed as the "all-Canadian" route, and arrived at Teslin Lake with two hundred head, worn out and thin from the rigours of the journey. They were slaughtered and butchered on the shore of the lake, and by mid-October, rafted out onto the tranquil waters for Dawson City. Unfortunately, the calm did not hold, and the rafts were dashed upon the rocky shore where the meat was lost.

The completion of the White Pass Railway put a quick end to the era of cattle drives into the Yukon. Jack Dalton had driven his first large herd over his trail for the Yukon market in 1897 and in 1906 newspapers heralded the final cattle drive of two hundred head, which passed through Dawson City en route to Fairbanks, Alaska.

Dead Horses on the Dalton Trail

When I received a new collection of photographs from a library in California, one of a horse bogged down in muskeg sparked something for me. Numerous references and accounts of horses, and the way they were treated, came together and moved me to write about them.

"From Skagway to Bennett they rotted in heaps. They died at the rocks, they were poisoned at the summit, and they starved at the lakes; they fell off the trail, what there was of it, and they went through it; in the river they drowned under their loads or were smashed to pieces against the boulders; they snapped their legs in the crevices and broke their backs falling backwards with their packs; in the sloughs they sank from freight or smothered in the slime; and they were disemboweled . . . men shot them, worked them to death and when they were gone, went back to the beach and bought more. Some did not bother to shoot them, stripping the saddles off and the shoes and leaving them where they fell. Their hearts turned to stone—those which did not break—and they became beasts, the men on the Dead Horse Trail." (Jack London, *The God of His Fathers*, 1914)

I pondered these immortal words from Jack London as I recently examined the bleached skull of a horse that lay beside the old Dalton Trail. After a hundred and ten years, it was surprising that such remains could still be found along this path to the gold rush.

The conditions on the Chilkoot Trail and the White Pass route have been well known for many years and similarly the Dalton Trail is littered with the corpses of horses that perished during the Klondike gold rush. They are testimony to the inhumanity of mankind toward these four-footed animals.

In 1896, the first herd of cattle was brought into the Yukon valley by Willis Thorp, a Juneau businessman, via the Dalton Trail, and for the next four years this was an important route for driving cattle to Dawson City. Thousands of horses, cattle and sheep travelled over this route to supply the demand for meat created by the ravenous miners in the Klondike.

Jack Dalton attempted to secure contracts to carry mail over this route, and even set up a pony express and pack-train business to carry freight and passengers 560 kilometres inland from Pyramid Harbor to Five Finger Rapids and back. Dalton brought in hundreds of horses for the business, but the enterprise failed.

The autumn of 1897 took a particularly brutal toll on the poor suffering animals. Planning to bring another herd in before freeze-up, Thorp, his son and their party departed Seattle aboard the *Farallon* on September 3 with ninety-two cattle, sixty horses, and three and one-half tonnes of supplies, headed for Pyramid Harbor and the trail they thought would be superior to the neighbouring Chilkoot or White Pass routes.

In his optimism and glow of success from his previous drive, Thorp paid no attention to the time of year. The herd hit the Chilkat Pass in early October and was caught in brutal weather.

They carried on for eighteen days, with horses dropping dead daily. The party didn't stop to remove the packs and valuable provisions, as there was no way they could add any load to the remaining animals. After thirty horses had perished in the bitter cold and drifting snow, the party divided; Thorp's son made a dash for the Yukon River with his winter supplies, and Thorp senior turned back from the summit at Chilkat Pass with the cattle and remaining horses. The trail was obscured by the deep drifting snow. Thorp led his party back toward the coast by following the dead horses, discarded harnesses, saddles and provisions they had abandoned on their journey in.

Israel Albert Lee, a gold seeker from Boston, was in a group following the Thorp party with twelve pack horses of their own. He didn't fare any better, although he travelled as far as Dalton's trading post. "All our horses are dead from exposure or starvation," he wrote from Dalton Post, "and we have packed about 1,600 pounds of food on our backs, for the last thirty-five miles, going ahead with what we could carry and then returning for more . . ." In the end, he too gave up and returned to the coast.

One beneficiary of the Thorp tragedy was Della Murray Banks. In the following summer of 1898, she accompanied her husband and a party of others over the Dalton Trail with dreams of Klondike riches. She was provided a horse but no saddle. Eventually they located an abandoned mule bit for her horse, then when they arrived at Glacier camp near the summit of the Chilkat Pass, exchanged it for a regular bridle found hanging in a tree. By the time they arrived at Dalton Post, she was riding on a fine saddle and with a good bridle, both cast-offs from others who had passed this way!

The trail was reasonably easy to follow, and Dalton and his crew had cut down trees to create corduroy through some of the marshy areas, yet horses still became trapped in the bogs. The bitter cold and starvation killed off the animals in the winter and the swamp got them in the summer, assuming mosquitoes didn't drive them mad first.

Of those who travelled to the Klondike over the Dalton Trail, horses suffered the worst of all. Here is one trapped in the boggy land along the route. Many were abandoned, worked to death, or shot. BANCROFT LIBRARY, BANC PIC 1961.016:16-ALB

William Shape and his partner stopped to help two men whose pack horse had become bogged down in one of the awful swamps. The four of them were able to get the poor animal out of the mire, but it was shaking, exhausted and unwilling to move on. A single shot from their revolver put the spent beast out of its misery.

Shape was no shining example of human compassion. He and his partner purchased a mare and a little sorrel from a cattle drive camped near Fort Selkirk to carry their supplies out of the Yukon over the Dalton Trail. Day after day they pressed on over the trail, showing little regard for the condition of the animals. The faithful little mare weakened daily, but they would not stop to allow her to regain her strength. Onward they pressed toward the coast. Nearing their goal, Shape noted that the mare had collapsed several times during the day, "but was doing nicely." Two days later, she could go no farther, so he shot her.

Ironically, Shape, who in the past fourteen months had walked two thousand eight hundred kilometres over every type of terrain and through all forms of weather, had gained nearly eight kilograms!

LEGENDARY PEOPLE

The Real-Life Legend of Klondike Joe Boyle

Pierre Berton once stated that Joe Boyle started his career as a bouncer in the Monte Carlo Saloon (Dawson City) and ended it as the lover of the Queen of Romania. Sounds pretty catchy, doesn't it? And if the story of Joe Boyle is even half true, he was a hero of epic proportions . . .

He was tall with broad shoulders and a winning smile, almost bigger than life they say. He was also a natural leader and unceasingly courageous, so it is fitting that the Historic Sites and Monuments Board of Canada declared him a person of national historic significance. A brass plaque stating this fact is mounted on a steel dredge bucket next to the Dredge Number 4 National Historic Site on Bonanza Creek near Dawson City. This dredge was one of the giant machines he built back in the early years after the gold rush.

Boyle grew up in Woodstock, Ontario, and then wanderlust took him in many directions before the Klondike. He was a merchant seaman, businessman and fight promoter before the gold rush lured him north in 1897. When he arrived, he saw an opportunity. While everyone else was stampeding to Dawson City, Boyle immediately turned around and headed to Ottawa, intent on securing a concession for large-scale mining.

He almost didn't make it. If it hadn't been for his grit, determination and leadership in the winter snows of the Dalton Trail, he and his companions

Joe Boyle wrestled control of the Canadian Klondyke Mining Corporation away from the Rothschilds and became known as "The King of the Klondike." YUKON ARCHIVES, WATT FAMILY FONDS, 92/57, PHOTO #110

would most certainly have perished. And this pattern of heroism is repeated throughout his life.

Boyle was successful in securing the rights to mining a large tract of land in the Klondike River valley. He then wrestled control of the Canadian Klondyke Mining Company from the powerful Rothschild family. By 1909, he was in charge of one of only two corporate mining giants in the Klondike and became known as "The King of the Klondike." His dredges were the biggest in the Yukon and almost certainly among the largest in the world.

Boyle did something else to put Dawson City on the map: he went after the Stanley Cup. His Dawson Nuggets challenged the Ottawa Silver Seven for the prize in 1905, but after an epic journey over snowy Yukon trails on foot, through the White Pass by rail, down the Pacific coast by boat, and across the continent by train, the exhausted Dawson Nuggets lost a record-breaking match with the Ottawa team. However, they still earned the right to have Dawson City's name engraved on the most famous hockey trophy in the world. It's the smallest town ever to compete for the cup.

With the outbreak of World War I in 1914, Joe left the Yukon for good. He stepped forward with an offer to finance and equip a machine-gun unit of fifty men for the Canadian Army. Too old at forty-seven to see active combat, he was given the honorary rank of Lieutenant-Colonel. When America joined the war in 1917, Boyle immediately signed up for the American Committee of Engineers. He embarked on a mission to get the Russian train system working. "Boyle's physical presence and determination, his ability to see to the heart of a problem and his willingness to use or ignore official channels to his purpose not only impressed his hosts," states a report to the Historic Sites and Monuments Board of Canada, "but made immediate improvements in the flow of food and ammunition to the Russian front." At Tarnapol, he helped restore order while under German attack, for which the Russians awarded him the Order of St. Vladimir.

In the winter of 1917–18 he became involved in supplying food to starving defeated Romanians, after which he arranged for the transfer of the crown jewels and national archives of Romania to Moscow to keep them out of German hands. He later made arrangements for their return.

Boyle moved from one exciting drama to another. He negotiated a treaty of peace between Russia and Romania; rescued sixty Romanian dignitaries held in Odessa and escaped with them to Romania via the Black Sea, operated an extensive spy network, and negotiated at the Versailles Peace Conference on behalf of Romania. And, yes, in all likelihood he became the lover of Queen Marie of Romania.

While never formally recognized in his lifetime by Canada for his wartime accomplishments, Boyle was decorated by several other countries, receiving the Distinguished Service Order of Great Britain, the French Croix de Guerre, the Russian Order of St. Vladimir, and the Order of the Star of Romania, to name a few.

Joe Boyle died in 1923 at the age of fifty-six after years of ill health in London, England. His remains were later repatriated to his home in Woodstock, Ontario, where they were interred with full military honours and provincial recognition in 1983. While still a young man when he died, he had packed more than a lifetime of adventure into his years.

Robert Service's Secret Love Life

After his first meeting with Constance MacLean in 1902, Robert Service tried to capture her attention by writing the lady a poem. In this way began a long and tortured romance between Robert Service and Miss MacLean of Vancouver...

A romance, you ask? The mild-mannered poet of the north? Wasn't he just a harmless clerk at the Bank of Commerce before he found fame as the champion of verse?

His biographers never mention his ardour for a pretty young Vancouverite he lovingly called Connie. James A. MacKay in his book *Vagabond of Verse* (1995) alluded to a mysterious "Cathy M" as the source of Service's affections. Only a more recent biography, Enid Mallory's *Under the Spell of the Yukon*, correctly pinpoints the object of his love interest and identifies her as the "C.M." to whom some of his early books are dedicated.

As a young man, Service led the footloose life of a hobo, wandering throughout the American West. He had settled down to life as a farm labourer and store clerk in Duncan, BC, when he first met Constance MacLean at a dance. She was visiting her uncle.

Service was immediately smitten, so it was natural that he would express his infatuation in verse. His writing to Miss MacLean never reached the

Robert Service's cabin in Dawson City, where he wrote many of his most memorable works, is now a national historic site operated by Parks Canada. MICHAEL GATES

excellence of his verse about the north. In fact the letters he wrote are not unlike those many of us wrote in the throes of young love.

From the beginning, the poet's letters expressed the roller-coaster emotions of a man head over heels for a young lady. She obviously wasn't impressed with the direction Service was taking (as a thirty-year-old store clerk with no career prospects) so he vowed: "I mean to follow the life you have indicated." MacLean was looking for a man of education and means to support her but Robert wasn't up to it. He attempted to please her by leaving his labouring job on the farm, enrolling in Vancouver College, an affiliate of McGill University, setting about to improve himself, but failing.

During the romance, Service once grovelled in apology for having written in a fit of jealousy because she was said to be corresponding with two other men. "I have repented in sack cloth and ashes for that letter," he confessed. He acknowledged that thinking of her made him blue, causing him to break down and cry "like a woman."

After his failed attempt at study, Service was spared starvation—and poverty—when he was offered a position at the Canadian Bank of Commerce in Kamloops. He was subsequently sent to Whitehorse in 1904. It is suggested that he took this faraway post to get some distance from Constance and try to forget her.

We know that for a period of time while Service was in Whitehorse, MacLean was employed as a governess in Atlin, BC, but there is nothing

Robert Service, here posing in front of his Dawson home, was a quiet, aging bank clerk with no future until his poems made him a wealthy man. YUKON ARCHIVES, GILLIS FAMILY FONDS, PHOTO #04533

to suggest that they saw each other during this time. We don't know what happened between Service and MacLean over the next few years as no letters from that period survived. But in 1908 after three years in Whitehorse he was sent Outside on mandatory paid leave for three months, a standard practice for bank employees serving in the Yukon.

In Vancouver their relationship was rekindled and when he was required to return to work, they had become engaged. This time he was being sent to Dawson City. His first book of verse had been published and was successful, so it must have been a dream come true for Service to be posted to the scene of the drama and excitement of the Klondike gold rush.

Service's letters to Miss MacLean from this period gushed with passion. Now, instead of "Miss Constance" or "dearest Constance," he greeted her with "my own beloved" and "my heart's dearest treasure." Instead of signing his letters Robert W. Service, he now used "Your adoring Bob." Cruising up the coast of Alaska on his way to his new posting, he admitted: "What a fool I was ever to agree to go back to the north." Further, he lamented, ". . . it can't be true that I'm not to see you tomorrow and feel your kisses . . . I will devote my life to you, only I want love from you, great all absorbing devotion, that's all I ask."

These are steamy words from the mild-mannered, self-effacing bank clerk. However, when he wrote his autobiography in later years not one word revealed his passionate correspondence with Miss Constance. The Klondike proved to be the more passionate and alluring mistress for Service. He was to be posted in Dawson City for eighteen months, after which he had planned to return to the arms of his sweetheart in Vancouver. But the Klondike stole him away. Service left his job with the bank on November 15, 1909, and instead of returning to Connie, moved into his own little cabin on Eighth Avenue overlooking the declining gold-rush community. There he wrote some of his greatest work. The rest, as they say, is history.

We don't know what happened between the two lovers after he was sent to Dawson City. There are no letters to fill the gap, nor are any of MacLean's letters to Service known to survive. Maybe she became impatient or perhaps Service lost interest. For a while, he may have been engaged to another woman in Dawson, a government stenographer, but that seems to have come to nothing. In 1912 Constance MacLean married Leroy Grant, a surveyor and railroad engineer based in Prince Rupert.

The Yukon's bard left the Klondike in 1912 and travelled widely around the globe. In Paris he met Germaine Bourgoin, a woman fifteen years his junior, and in June 1913 they were married. The union lasted for the remaining forty-five years of Service's life. From all accounts, those years were filled with contentment for Yukon's renowned author.

Service never saw Constance MacLean again. Ironically, he crossed paths with her husband during World War I, but it is not known if Service knew who he was. Service kept in touch with other members of her family, so it is likely that over the years, he heard stories of his former love. I can only imagine what feelings flashed through him at such times. Was it regret? Was she his one and only true love? Did he long for her embrace? Or did Service dismiss his relationship with her as a failed love affair and move on to a stellar career as a poet and novelist, never to look back? Service's legacy survives in his many volumes of verse and other writings. His little cabin in Dawson City has become a national shrine, where every summer visitors are entertained with readings of his works. And the love letters? They are securely stored in the archives at Queen's University in Kingston, Ontario.

The Pioneer Woman of Squaw Creek

She was an American woman who gave up a life of high society, comfort and privilege for the tough existence of a miner in the wilds of the Yukon and northern British Columbia . . .

When Europeans first entered the Yukon, they found a harsh and challenging environment. The women of the late-Victorian era were defined within a multitude of social customs and constraints. They were not considered to be up to the rigours of wilderness life. Yet there were a few who defied the conventions of the time and proved they were as capable of meeting the challenge as any man.

Arabelle Frances Patchen was one of these women. She was born in St. Paul, Minnesota, on August 10, 1874. Her family moved to Spokane when she was twelve years old, then on to Coeur d'Alene a year later. She was only eighteen years old when she married an older prosecuting attorney in Spokane and became "an ornament to Spokane society."

She was small and slim, with a beautiful oval face and engaging gaze. In her early days as a trophy wife, she was elegantly attired in fashionable gowns. Later, as a seasoned veteran of the north, she opted for the rough-and-ready garb of the outdoors.

She might have lived a life of comfort for the rest of her years had she not participated in a charity fundraiser and scandalized her conservative

Frances Muncaster, centre, is shown in front of the cabin on her Squaw Creek claim during the 1930s. YUKON ARCHIVES, MADGE MANDY COLLECTION 95/51, PHOTO #1

husband by riding bareback into the arena wearing a fluffy pale-blue knee-length skirt over pink tights. After three years of marriage, Arabelle Frances Allen moved on.

The attractive, petite woman drew men like a magnet and one of them, Thomas Noyes, the son of a Montana mining tycoon, married her. Like thousands of others, the newlyweds headed for the Klondike, spending a winter in Skagway, followed by prospecting at the foot of a glacier and ultimately arriving in Nome, Alaska, in 1900.

Unlike many, Frances Noyes and her husband stayed in the north in a full partnership, becoming involved in numerous ventures with varying success. At one time, Frances was the toast of Monte Carlo in Europe, but eventually the couple was wiped out financially, leaving only memories of "perilous trips, lost trails, and climbs over glaciers."

They adopted a half-Inuit girl named Bonnie in 1905. In 1914, they stampeded to the Chisana region along the Alaska–Yukon border hoping to recover their fortunes, but met only failure. Tom died in 1916.

Frances, now a widow in her forties, remained in Alaska, managing a cannery store. Here, a man fifteen years her junior fell in love with her, and in June 1919 she married Bill Muncaster, a surveyor. For their honeymoon they set off with Bonnie over two glaciers to the head of the White River through deep snows and temperatures so low that the mercury had retreated into the bulb. They spent that winter in a cabin on Wellesley Lake, hunting, fishing and presumably keeping warm.

Her husband Bill once wrote in admiration: "[I] Have seen her day after day cover 20 to 25 miles on snow shoes [and] just took it like an ever[y] day chore." At a time of life when other women might be thinking of relaxing, Frances Muncaster was only just beginning her adventures.

On one trip driving horses from Wellesley Lake to Burwash in 1923, her adoring husband claimed, ". . . it was so cold our thermometer went to the bulb at 56 below and stayed there for some ten day. But we had to keep going for we were out there us two 100 mile or so from nowhere but she loved it." For years, they continued their quest for gold in the southwest Yukon.

In 1927, when Frances was in her fifties, she and Bill were living in Washington State. Visiting the Muncaster family in Seattle, a nephew overheard her having an emotional conversation with Bill in the next room. Frances was crying and emphatic that she wanted to return to the north. Her husband promised to do so just as soon as they had a grubstake together.

When word reached her through the moccasin telegraph in 1927 of gold being discovered by Paddy Duncan at Squaw Creek on the Alaska–British Columbia border, she immediately set off on her own to seek fortune; her husband Bill following soon after. She staked a claim on Squaw Creek and was soon appointed by the government as the mining recorder for the district. It was here that she and her husband continued to mine for the next twenty years.

And it was a hard go. Her nephew described their trip back to Squaw Creek in 1928. They relayed their supplies by dog team, caching their gear and then backtracking through the snows to bring in the next load. They were attacked by wolves and stalked by wolverines, and when it became too warm during the day to travel through the melting snows, were forced to wait for the cool of the evening to travel over the frozen crust. When her husband, bringing supplies in by horse, joined them, they crossed the swollen Tatshenshini River by holding on to their horses' tails for dear life. They recovered thirty-five dollars in gold per day at Squaw Creek, but due to the high cost of goods in this remote region, this was only enough to carry them from one year to the next.

Author Madge Mandy described an encounter with Frances at Squaw Creek in the early 1930s: "She looked beyond middle age . . . with silvered brown hair and a very feminine fragile appearance. Her pretty face was lined with character and her outgoing personality had warmth like a friendly embrace . . ."

At age sixty, she was teaching a younger man how to pack supplies by dog team from Haines to Squaw Creek through the thawing snows of the Chilkat summit. But as the years advanced, her energy finally started to fade and the mining trips became shorter and less arduous. Following a remarkable life, she died of a heart attack at Haines, Alaska, at age seventy-eight in 1952.

Martha Black was a Woman of the North

When I look back over the accounts of pioneer women included in this volume, I realize many were American. This selection was not by design. Is it possible that they were more adventurous?

Martha's husband, MP George Black, was sick in 1935 and in the veterans' hospital in London, Ontario. An election was looming and he was not going to recover in time to campaign for his seat in parliament. So Martha wrote to Prime Minister R.B. Bennett and told him that they had both always been strong Conservative supporters and that with a little financial support she could run for the Yukon seat instead. Bennett agreed. She ran, and won the seat in the 1935 election and held it for five years. George recovered and regained it in the following election. In the Yukon, it was said that there were two political parties: the Liberals and the Blacks.

Martha Louise Black was only the second woman to hold a seat in the Canadian House of Commons, and she was born American to boot. During her term in office, she continually alluded to her husband's return in the next election, and through her correspondence, showed her loyalty to that cause. Although the Conservatives did not gain a majority in 1935, Martha won the Yukon riding for them, as her husband had done many times before. Between them, George and Martha Black held the Yukon seat in parliament for three decades, from 1921 till 1949.

Martha Munger was born to a wealthy Chicago family in 1866 and grew up in upper middle-class comfort. She married Will Amon Purdy at the age of twenty-one and became occupied with the task of rearing two sons, but chafed under the restrictions imposed on her by society and family. Despite being pregnant for the third time, Martha Purdy was quite ready to go north to the Klondike for adventure when gold was discovered. She parted with her husband on the way to Dawson City (they eventually divorced) and continued in the company of her brother George Merrick Munger, Jr. She gave birth to her third son, Lyman, in a tiny log cabin upriver from Dawson City in the dead of winter 1899.

During an era when men traditionally ran the show, Martha—backed by her family—managed a sawmill in Dawson City for several years. It was through her business that she met and eventually, in the summer of 1904, married George Black, a local lawyer who was active in politics.

"I am a firm believer," said Martha in her autobiography, *My Ninety Years*, "in the principle that married couples, from the beginning, should be in complete harmony in religion, in country, and in politics. So I immediately became an Anglican, an Imperialist, and a Conservative."

She and her husband became a political dynasty that lasted half a century. George was an active campaigner who ran for the territorial assembly, and was elected for several terms.

Martha stood behind him throughout his career, helping with his campaigns by organizing dinners, social functions, attending political rallies, and eventually by holding his seat in parliament for him.

Martha Black did it all: climbed the Chilkoot Trail, bore a son in her Yukon log cabin, ran a business, wrote a book about herself and became the second woman elected to the House of Commons. YUKON ARCHIVES, MUNGER FAMILY FONDS 78/112, PHOTO #4

When George was appointed Commissioner of the Yukon in 1912, the couple moved into the Commissioner's Residence and kept up an active social life as leaders in the community. Four years later, when George went overseas during World War I, Martha accompanied him to London as the only female passenger on a troop ship. Throughout the war, while George was stationed with his troops and then shipped to the trenches of France, she remained in England, making frequent lectures and speeches about the Yukon, attending social functions, and providing comfort to homesick Yukon soldiers who came to visit her.

After the war, they returned to Vancouver and Martha continued to support George's political ambitions. After a close but unsuccessful run in provincial politics in British Columbia, George was elected to parliament as Yukon's MP in 1921.

The couple travelled constantly between Dawson City and Ottawa, relying on boat and train rather than jet to get them there. Throughout the next thirty years, they entertained and became widely popular among parliamentarians. When George became Speaker of the House in 1930, their hectic social schedule increased and included entertaining royalty who visited Canada.

During her term in parliament, Martha repeatedly made it clear that her political ambition was to keep her husband's seat in the House of Commons until his return. George was re-elected in March of 1940. When the Conservative leader Dr. R.J. Mannion lost his parliamentary seat, Martha hastened to put forth George's name as an interim leader, but it came to nothing. They continued their busy schedule until George left politics for good in 1953. Martha died in 1957, in her ninety-second year.

What was she like? Like many women who chose to move to the north, she went against the grain of social standards of the time. She was staunchly egalitarian, and while George was commissioner, their doors were open to people of all stripes. Her father used to tell her that she could, someday, become the president's wife—or his servant—and he wanted her to know how to do both equally well.

At one of her teas, she had her washerwoman's daughter "pass," an honour usually reserved for the social elite. When challenged about this, she responded that her father was a washerman (he made his fortune in the laundry business in Chicago). She could handily drop names where the circumstances allowed. She had been educated in finishing school, and had rubbed shoulders with the elite of society.

Martha Black was well suited to a life in the Yukon. A non-conformist with a privileged upbringing, she yearned for the unconventional and the exciting. After participating in the most colourful odyssey in Canadian history, she adopted the north as her home and never looked back. For the next six decades, she made her indelible mark on the Yukon.

Martha Black was more than a socialite. She elevated her passion for Yukon flora to a high art by publishing a small book on the subject, eventually becoming a Fellow of the Royal Geographical Society. She established the first chapter of the Imperial Order of the Daughters of the Empire (IODE) in the Yukon. At age seventy, she jointly authored her autobiography. In 1946, she was awarded the Order of the British Empire (O.B.E.). She was an avid booster of the Yukon and frequently spoke on the subject, often illustrated with photographic slides taken by her husband.

In 1987, the Historic Sites and Monuments Board of Canada recognized her contribution to Canada, and a plaque was unveiled in her honour at Dawson City. On it, her participation in the Klondike gold rush, her short business career, her interest in Yukon flora and her standing as the second woman elected to the Canadian parliament are identified as reasons for her designation as a person of national significance.

Early Gold Recorders Kept Order on the Creeks

Gold miners were an independent lot who had an inherent mistrust of government rules and bureaucracy, yet even they seemed to understand the need for someone to sort out the conflicting interests that would arise when claims are staked on disputed ground. Before the government came on the scene, this responsibility fell upon an individual sanctioned by the local miners. This time-honoured system of miners' committees came to an end in 1896. The story of the showdown between the miners and the Mounties at Glacier Creek is described earlier in this volume.

One hundred and twenty-five years ago, no more than a dozen prospectors saw through the long, cold winter in the Yukon River basin. For ten years, there had been a mere handful of them in the country, but in 1882, for the first time, parties of miners reached Fort Reliance, located a few kilometres below the future site of Dawson City.

During that winter, the miners convened a meeting, the first of its kind in the Yukon valley, to establish rules about the use of water for mining and allowable sizes for claims. Jack McQuesten, who ran the tiny trading post at Fort Reliance, was elected the first mining recorder. In McQuesten's own personal recollections, he does not spell out exactly what his responsibilities as mining recorder were.

The early miners and prospectors lived in a political vacuum, a wilderness devoid of boundaries. As such, the area had neither constitution nor a formal body to enforce one. Thus, they implemented rules previously established in the camps of former gold rushes and managed their affairs under an anarchistic democracy called the miners' committee.

These committees were flexible and efficient. When gold was discovered on Fortymile River, a miners' committee decided that each claim was to be roughly 460 metres in length. The next season, however, when the Fortymile was flooded with prospectors, the committee reduced the claim size to ninety metres in an effort to deal with the potential for conflict and ensure that everybody was able to take out enough gold to pay for their grubstake.

This method of administration was practical, but it also had a dark side. As the population of miners in the Yukon valley grew, the potential for these committees to go awry increased, especially when liquor was involved. Disputes heard by miners' committees often resulted in patently unfair judgments.

In 1895, more than twenty years after the first prospectors arrived, the North-West Mounted Police came on the scene. The Mounties were assigned many responsibilities during their posting at Forty Mile; among them the role of first official mining recorder in the Yukon fell to the commanding officer, Inspector Charles Constantine.

Constantine's duties in this regard were clear: he was to apply the regulations pertaining to staking and recording of placer claims according to rules set out by the Canadian government. Many of the miners on the creeks were ready for a change, and

Inspector Charles Constantine of the North-West Mounted Police became the first government-appointed mining recorder in the Yukon in 1895. RCMP HISTORICAL COLLECTION, CATALOGUE NUMBER 1934.15.6

those who weren't, quickly moved to Circle, Alaska, beyond the reach of British justice.

In the summer of 1896, there was a dispute over non-payment of wages, and Inspector Constantine dispatched a dozen armed officers and men to settle the dispute. This was the first time a decision of a miners' committee was overturned and it foretold the end of an era, but not before one final miners' meeting was held a few weeks later on a tiny tributary of the Yukon, eighty kilometres above Forty Mile.

In mid-August of 1896, George Washington Carmack and his First Nation relatives Skookum Jim Mason (known as Keish in his Tagish community) and Dawson Charley found a significant showing of placer gold on a minor tributary of the Klondike River named Rabbit Creek. They had been invited by Canadian prospector Robert Henderson to visit him on a tributary of Hunker Creek called Gold Bottom. On or about August 17, as they were returning to the fish camp they had set up near the mouth of the Klondike River, the three men discovered promising prospects and staked four contiguous claims along this small stream. Carmack and Charley made their way to Forty Mile to file with the Mounted Police while Jim remained behind to guard the ground and begin working the site. Joe Ladue, who operated a trading post on an island in the Yukon River near the mouth of the Sixtymile River, was optimistically steering incoming prospectors in the direction of Henderson's promising claim on Gold Bottom. Some of those headed in that direction encountered Carmack and Charley and when told of the new find amended their plans and headed up Rabbit Creek instead.

Carmack also announced his discovery in the town of Forty Mile. This had the electric effect of clearing out the community in short order while Carmack was presenting himself to Inspector Constantine to file his claim. Unfortunately, Carmack had thrown down all his gold in Bill McPhee's saloon when he announced his find, and was unable to present even a sample to Constantine as proof that he had in fact found it on his new claim. As required in the regulations, Constantine sent Carmack back to his prospect to recover the requisite gold, and it was therefore almost six weeks after the original staking that he was in fact able to file his claims.

While Carmack was in Forty Mile, prospectors had made their way up to the newly discovered gold stream. Six days after the Carmack trio had staked, two dozen miners assembled on a bench overlooking the creek and convened a miners' meeting. They renamed the creek Bonanza, and its main tributary Eldorado, and appointed a Nova Scotian named Dave McKay to act as the recorder. Using a length of rope, McKay measured out each man's claim and listed them on paper.

When the stakes are high, as they were on Bonanza Creek, the work of the mining recorder must become an exact science. Problems were created by the varied and inexact knowledge of mining regulations and the antics of the prospectors who stampeded to Bonanza. The rope that was used to measure the claims was not properly measured, so all the claims were shorter than allowed. Another claim proved to be almost double the legal length, the result, it was alleged, of being measured out in darkness. Another was so poorly measured that the lower post on it proved to be four metres above the upper one, leaving the owner with four metres less than nothing.

Many claims were staked in the absence of the reputed owner, and in one case a deputation of miners relocated one man's claim six kilometres farther down the stream. Chaos reigned over the creeks, and dealing with these disorderly circumstances was beyond McKay's capabilities. You can only imagine the turmoil that would have resulted had the confusion not been resolved.

The miners turned to the one man they all trusted to unravel the confusion: William Ogilvie, the Canadian government surveyor. Early in 1897, Ogilvie applied his technical skills and knowledge of the regulations—along with the wisdom of Solomon—to sort things out. In the end, he created order out of chaos with his decisions accepted by all without dispute.

The days of the miners' committee were at an end. The appointment and responsibilities of the mining recorder could no longer be a spur-of-the-moment affair. It was time for the government to take over the job.

Bill Gates: Klondike Casanova
or Gold-Rush Gouger?

There weren't any takers for "Swiftwater" Bill Gates when the notable Klondike character stepped out in Butte, Montana, just before Christmas of 1904 looking for a wife—"a real nice, good girl, who will really care for him and not his money."

Swiftwater wasn't ugly and was a rather dapper dresser in his Prince Albert coat, top hat, white shirt with a diamond stickpin in his tie, and starched collar. He was of medium height and powerfully built, with bright, active eyes and a handsome bearded face.

Bill wasn't poor either. He had become a millionaire during the Klondike stampede, then doubled his good fortune on a claim on Cleary Creek near Fairbanks. Everywhere he went he seemed to find more of the yellow metal.

His undoing, perhaps, was that he liked the ladies—arguably a little too much.

In 1896, twenty-eight-year-old Bill Gates was an insignificant dishwasher in a saloon in Circle City, Alaska. Like many others, he heard the siren call of the Klondike and partnered with six other men leasing unlucky Claim Number 13 on Eldorado Creek. They sank shaft after shaft, each one barren and dispiriting, until Bill found himself alone to pursue the yellow metal. He finally sank a shaft that hit the pay streak. Suddenly, he was one of the richest men in the Klondike, worth hundreds of thousands (millions in today's dollars).

From inconspicuous roots, he became one of the liveliest and most visible men in Dawson City. Everywhere he went, he drew attention to himself with wild and extravagant behaviour. He gambled with a passion and became well known for making large, impulsive bets.

And, oh, how he liked the ladies, and one in particular. Nineteen-year-old Gussie Lamore was an entertainer in Circle City who had followed opportunity to Dawson. Bill wanted her at any price, at one point actually offering Gussie her own weight in gold if she would marry him. When he caught her stepping out on him, his revenge was equally colourful. Gussie loved eggs, and when Bill saw her with another man, he vowed to deny her that indulgence. At the height of the winter of 1897 eggs were hard to find and those that were available were gamey and aromatic, but Gussie loved them anyway. Bill bought up the entire supply in Dawson and was forevermore known as "The Knight of the Golden Omelette."

The number of eggs involved and the price paid for them varies from one

"Swiftwater" Bill Gates (seated), with his wife Bera behind him, his mother-in-law to the left and partner Joe Boyle to the right, at his cabin on Quartz Creek. The woman to the far left is unidentified. YUKON ARCHIVES, NATIONAL ARCHIVES OF CANADA COLLECTION, PHOTO #00602

account to the next. Gussie had the final word on this episode in a newspaper interview a few years later: "I went down to the store to buy some eggs. Lordy how I wanted some eggs for breakfast. Well Bill was in the store when I goes in. He sees I want the eggs and while I'm talking with the clerk, see, he buys up the whole consignment at $1 apiece. Then he says to me, 'Now, my dear, if you want eggs for breakfast, come home where you belong.' Well, say, I was just dying for them eggs and I came to my milk like a lady. I goes home with Bill."

Bill chased Gussie all the way to San Francisco in the fall of 1897, but as it turned out she couldn't marry him as she was already married with a three-year-old child! So he wed her younger sister Grace instead. He indulged his new bride with a $15,000 mansion in Oakland and showered her with gifts. The marriage was short-lived, however, as Grace proved a pale substitute for Gussie and knew it. Grace stated she was prepared to stand aside and let Bill fulfill his passion for her sister. "This will be no sacrifice on my part," she said, "for I hate the very ground he walks on and abhor him and his name." Soon after, they were divorced.

Everywhere that Bill went he spent money at an amazing pace. Woe to those who invested with him for they seldom saw a penny of it again. Among these unfortunates was his soon-to-be mother-in-law Iola Beebe.

It wasn't long before he was married again, to Bera Beebe. According to her mother, Bera was a plump sixteen-year-old, with deliciously pink cheeks and great big blue eyes. At one point, Swiftwater took Bera and their son on a trip to Washington, DC, where he abandoned her just as she was expecting their second child. Back in Montana, Bill caught up with Gussie once more, and this time surprised his long-time love interest and the media by running off with another Lamore sister, Belle. She was also known as Nellie and nicknamed "Nellie the Pig" because, it was said, she had once tried to bite off a bartender's ear. Bill didn't marry Belle, as far as we know, but it wasn't long before the wedding bells were chiming again. In June 1901, while still married to Bera, he tied the knot with his fourteen-year-old stepniece Adelina Boyle (also referred to as Kitty) in Chehalis, Washington.

Now a bigamist, Gates was arrested in San Francisco for abducting his niece—but no one was willing to press charges and soon he was up to his antics once again. Eventually divorcing Bera, he remarried Kitty, making her both wife number three and four. By 1906, they too divorced and he found himself in bankruptcy court.

He must have had something special. Before committing suicide, second-wife Bera vowed undying love for her runaway husband and claimed she wished to marry him again. Gussie admitted a lasting soft spot for him, too.

Bill lacked either good judgment or common sense, or both, for two years later, in 1908—now almost forty years old and burning through his third fortune—he married again, this time to eighteen-year-old Sadelle Mercer at Coeur d'Alene, Idaho.

By 1915, he added another credit to his reputation, that of deadbeat dad. While in Seattle that year, preparing to sail to Peru for more adventure, he was arrested by his persistent ex-mother-in-law Beebe. This time the charge was child abandonment. I don't know what happened in this case, but can tell you that Bill eventually made it to Peru where he lived out his remaining years still looking for gold, until he was murdered on February 21, 1937.

So I ask you—if you were a decent woman looking for a good husband, would you be among those many women who chose "Swiftwater" Bill Gates?

Is Father Judge a Forgotten Hero?

It is an unfortunate truth that acts of kindness and good deeds go unrecognized while extravagant, outrageous, violent and lawless behaviour receives too much attention in our daily lives. When I googled Swiftwater Bill, for instance, I got over 13,000 hits. A similar search for Father William Judge yielded only nine . . .

"If it bleeds, it leads" is one of journalism's golden rules. Newspapers, television and the Internet are clogged with articles depicting murder, tragedy, violence and crime. I have yet to see a newspaper run a headline claiming "Today, Only Good Deeds Were Performed."

I suppose that is why Father William Judge, a Jesuit priest, had so little newspaper ink devoted to his acts of kindness and good service to the public during the Klondike stampede. Father William Judge was well known for his acts of charity and compassion during the gold rush. He stands out as the most selfless man in the greed-inspired phenomenon that was the Klondike.

William Henry Judge was born into a religious family in Baltimore, Maryland, April 28, 1850. In addition to William, four of his siblings also entered holy orders. As a youth he was frail and sickly, but he persevered and at age twenty-five embarked on years of study and teaching in the Jesuit order. Finally, in 1890, at the age of forty, he volunteered for service in the Alaskan mission. After a journey that lasted several months, he arrived at Holy Cross

Mission, the principal Jesuit centre on the Yukon River, where he joined the Father Superior, two brothers, and three Sisters of St. Ann, who taught fifty schoolchildren.

Judge had acquired many useful skills before he became a priest, including those of carpenter, cabinetmaker, blacksmith and baker. These skills were put to good use and he soon earned the respect of his colleagues at Holy Cross. After two years there he was assigned to a smaller mission at Nulato where he spent his time teaching Native children in their own language, constructing a church, and travelling widely to visit both white and aboriginal people in the region. He was happy and content with his assignment.

Father Judge, "The Saint of Dawson," is recognized by the Historic Sites and Monuments Board of Canada for his work in Dawson City during the gold rush. AUTHOR'S COLLECTION

Orders then reached him from the Father Superior to establish a mission at the small mining town of Forty Mile, hundreds of kilometres up the Yukon River. His fortitude was tested at his new post, where he alone served the spiritual needs of the Catholic community. "No doubt," he said, "the hardest part will be to be alone for ten months, with no communication whatever with the other Fathers; but I hope it will be alone with God." The challenge for the missionary was formidable because the "leaderless legion" of miners had little concern for anything but the search for gold.

Father Judge noted: ". . . everybody is looking for gold, some finding it and some getting nothing, a few becoming rich, but the greater number only making a living, and all working very, very hard. You would be astonished to see the amount of hard work that men do here in the hope of finding gold . . . O if men would only work for the kingdom of heaven with a little of that wonderful energy, how many saints we would have."

The low water on the Yukon River made it hard for him to get to Forty Mile in the first place. Then, when he was reassigned to Circle in 1896, the same conditions prevented him from leaving. In Forty Mile, his diaries reveal, he kept up a rigorous routine of visits to the sick, the needy and the miners out on the remote creeks.

He was well positioned to provide aid when gold was discovered on Rabbit Creek, soon to be renamed Bonanza. He spent the winter tending to his dwindling Forty Mile flock. In March of 1897 he followed them to Dawson, "... a solitary, feeble old man with a single sled rope over his shoulder, and a single dog helping the load along..."

Judge had secured three acres of land near the north end of Dawson. Once he was settled he set about building a church, a residence and a hospital. The latter, completed on August 20, 1897, was sadly needed in the forthcoming months. With the harsh climate, poor nutrition and deplorable sanitation in the new town, the hospital was in immediate demand.

Father Judge built the first hospital in Dawson City, shown under construction in the background. The tent may have served as a temporary hospital. LIBRARY OF CONGRESS, PPMSCA 08696

Father Judge built the first Catholic church in Dawson City during the gold rush. AUTHOR'S COLLECTION

He was soon tending to twenty patients a day, rising to fifty in the winter. During the typhoid epidemic in the fall of 1898 he served 135 patients daily. This dramatic increase made necessary the construction of an addition to the hospital. Until reinforcements arrived, Judge tended to his congregation single-handedly, in addition to supervising the construction, raising funds and managing the hospital.

Father Judge dedicated himself selflessly to his work. He spent hours "cheering and comforting the sick and consoling the dying." His kindness and generosity knew no religious boundaries. When the new church burned to the ground in June 1898, he immediately set about raising funds and managing the construction of a larger replacement, which was complete within ten weeks.

When reinforcements arrived in the late summer of 1898, he was able to hand over the responsibility for nursing and care of the sick to the Sisters of St. Ann and the services in the new church to the Oblates, and he continued his dedicated work as hospital chaplain and administrator.

For two years, he had laboured without thought or concern for himself, devoted solely to the care of others. Exhausted from his labour, in early

January of 1899 he fell ill and for days battled pneumonia until he finally succumbed on January 16.

The sadness of his passing was shared by the entire community, regardless of religious persuasion. Both his spiritual work and contributions to his fellow man were widely recognized. During all of his trials he exhibited a calm and serenity that contrasted with the frenzy and obsession that surrounded him as thousands of gold seekers poured into the area. He was, perhaps, "the only person in Dawson who sacrificed himself totally to the needs of others for no earthly reward." It was for this above all else that he became known as "The Saint of Dawson."

If you go to the north end of Dawson today, you will find a quiet clearing overlooking the Yukon River very near where his great works took place. It is here that he was laid to rest. Nearby, a plaque mounted on a huge block of stone by the Historic Sites and Monuments Board of Canada recognizes his contributions to the physical and spiritual well-being of the miners of the Klondike.

The Case of the Drunken Diplomat

In earlier days, the press was far more circumspect in the way it handled political affairs than it is today. Reporters would cover the political scene without delving into the personal side of prominent political figures.

Times have changed, of course, and today every aspect of a politician's life seems to be open to scrutiny. Adultery? Bribery? Drunkenness? It's all fair game now. Former president Bill Clinton could attest to that fact. But when the outrageous behaviour of a prominent diplomat and public figure in Dawson City was exposed during the gold rush, he really had to provoke the press to get himself placed under the media microscope.

During the height of the gold rush, the majority of the population of Dawson City and the goldfields were American. The Fourth of July was as big a celebration as the Queen's birthday. It is not surprising that the United States established a consulate in the heart of town.

A consul, according to the dictionary, is defined as "an official appointed by the government of a country to look after its business interests in a foreign city, and to assist citizens of that country living there." Consulates are usually placed in cities of consequence, which reflects the prominence of Dawson City during the gold rush. Despite the importance of the United

James McCook, the American consul, made the mistake of challenging the *Daily Klondike Nugget* in Dawson City. *DAILY KLONDIKE NUGGET*, ARTHUR BUEL CARTOON

States consul in Dawson City and the reticence of the press a century ago, the American-owned local newspaper, the *Daily Klondike Nugget*, chose to report on the incident of the drunken diplomat.

The story began with Thomas Fawcett, the Gold Commissioner, whom the *Nugget* vilified rightly or wrongly, for corruption related to the staking of claims on Dominion Creek eighty kilometres south of Dawson City. The *Nugget* hounded Fawcett even after he was demoted. When Fawcett finally left Dawson City in the spring of 1899 a farewell dinner was organized and US consul J.C. McCook attended, eulogizing the exiting Fawcett much to the disgust of the *Nugget*.

McCook responded to a tart editorial published by the *Nugget* on March 22, 1899, commenting on the article point by point. The little American rag replied by attacking the consul in very eloquent prose, concluding that "The Colonel [McCook] is a gentleman and a judge of whiskey, but some kind friend ought to whisper in his ear that writing letters is not his forte, but his weakness."

On April 1 the *Nugget* further responded by calling McCook a "buffoon" and a "fun-maker" and criticizing the grammar in the consul's letter.

The *Nugget* clarified in its April 5 edition that the April 1 article was not a prank and followed in its April 8 edition with an Arthur Buel cartoon that depicted the consul as a barefoot schoolboy tearfully completing his first grammar lesson, which was a letter to the editor of the *Nugget*. A few days later, the pot of controversy was stirred some more. Sporting a front-page cartoon of the consul drunkenly dancing on a flag-draped coffin labelled "US

TO GO OUT WITH THE ICE IN THE SPRING.

When the American consul went on a bender, he was attacked by the *Daily Klondike Nugget* and ridiculed by cartoonist Arthur Buel. *DAILY KLONDIKE NUGGET*, ARTHUR BUEL CARTOON

Dignity," the newspaper also published a notice that McCook had brought suit against it for damage to his reputation.

The gloves were now off. The *Nugget*, hesitant to publish anything about an official's private life, became incensed by McCook's behaviour at the Phoenix dance hall on April 6. McCook arrived at 3:00 a.m. in a drunken state with none other than Diamond Tooth Gertie Lovejoy, one of Dawson's colourful dance-hall characters, on his arm. Inside the Phoenix, he continued drinking. At one point, the patriotic McCook was brawling with a Canadian patron. They almost crashed through the front window and later tumbled to the dance-hall floor where a less-than-sober porter attempted to separate them. McCook then pinned a small American flag to the seat of his own pants, and before a shocked crowd challenged Pete, the night porter, to kick the flag. Sometime between 7:00 and 8:00 a.m., he was escorted out the rear of the premises into Paradise Alley where the very tipsy consul unsuccessfully tried to enter one of the back-street "cigar stores." During the gold rush, the term "cigar store" was euphemistically used to reference the small cribs where prostitutes plied their trade in the alley just behind Front Street. Next, on hands and knees, McCook entered the Rochester Hotel where his request for whiskey was refused. Half an hour later, he stumbled out the door and made his way back to the consulate across the street.

The repentant consul later stated his version of events in a letter to Washington, claiming he had been framed by an anarchist editor. He explained that he had not crawled on hands and knees but had merely slipped on the ice and quickly returned to his feet.

In a scathing editorial titled "Eagle's Drooped Wings," the *Nugget* stated the consul had brought shame on his flag and country and should step down from his position. McCook retaliated by filing a charge of defamatory libel against the *Nugget*, which responded April 19 with a cartoon of a still-drunken, pointy-eared consul lying amongst the garbage on the Yukon River ice awaiting spring breakup. In subsequent issues, the *Nugget* continued to campaign for McCook's removal from office.

The libel case went before a judge and jury. The *Nugget* won the case and gleefully reported every detail in its June 3 edition. Having already been embarrassed multiple times by the newspaper, McCook had again been exposed to ridicule before a packed courtroom as witness after witness, including several dance-hall girls, stood up to testify about the goings on at the Phoenix saloon that fateful April morning.

After the trial was over, the *Nugget* closed the book on the "McCook fight."

"If Consul McCook listens to the advice of those who really are his friends," stated the newspaper, "he will retire before the facts in the case are presented at Washington." McCook departed Dawson in late September, but returned later for two more summers of consular service.

A final thought: If a prominent public official pokes the media with a stick it will respond. If McCook had not provoked the *Nugget* with letters and lawsuits, the original article would have been forgotten soon after it was published. Thankfully he didn't. His antics made for plenty of entertaining reading. I'll bet he sold a lot of newspapers, too!

A Canadian Poser Governed Alaska
for Five Years

My wife, Kathy, and I travelled to Skagway, Alaska, in July of 2009. Talking with Judy Munns, director of the Skagway Museum about Klondike stampeders who had come from the maritime provinces of Canada, we learned about one Canadian who passed himself off as an American and was appointed Governor of Alaska . . . until he was found out. This was too good a story not to be told.

There's Milli Vanilli—remember them? They won the 1990 Grammy for Best New Artist—and then were exposed as frauds and discredited. Their Grammy was rescinded.

There was Grey Owl, also known as Wa-sha-quon-asin, an Ojibwa who had been a trapper, wilderness guide and forest ranger. He wrote extensively and was known as a champion of the Canadian conservation movement. But Grey Owl was a fraud too, actually an Englishman named Archibald Stansfeld Belaney who had always wanted to live a Native lifestyle. He wrote a number of successful books and went on speaking tours in Britain in the 1930s. After his death in 1938 though, he was exposed as an imposter. It set back the conservation cause in Canada by many years.

Then there was J.F.A. Strong, governor of Alaska.

Starting in the late 1880s, John Franklin Alexander Strong worked for a variety of newspapers in Spokane, Bellingham, Tacoma and Seattle. In 1896, while editor of the *Tacoma Ledger*, he married Annie Hall from Seattle. Annie was an accomplished musician who spent five years studying music in Paris and Berlin, and then taught music and German at the University of Washington before she married. Fifteen years his junior, she became his constant companion and partner in his newspaper and other activities for the next thirty-three years.

Like thousands of others, Strong was caught up in the excitement of the Klondike gold rush and he headed north with his bride in 1897. Arriving in Skagway too late in the season to travel farther to Dawson City, Strong hired on as the associate editor of the newly founded *Skagway News*. He had plenty to write about.

The law-abiding citizens of Skagway were fed up with the antics of Jefferson "Soapy" Smith, leader of a gang of thieves, thugs and confidence men that had terrorized Skagway for several months. Strong quickly became the voice of citizens who objected to Smith's criminal activities. When a Smith emissary appeared in Strong's office to offer a bribe of one hundred dollars a day to lay off the criticism, Strong refused and even increased his attacks on the gang, joining forces with a number of others to form a vigilance committee to take action.

When Soapy tried to crash a mass meeting held by the committee on the Skagway waterfront, he was gunned down by Frank Reid. It was later uncovered that J.A. Hornsby, editor of the competing *Daily Alaskan*, was in Smith's pocket. Hornsby was run out of town along with the remaining members of the gang.

In 1899, Strong and his wife

This distinguished gentleman was J.F.A. Strong, governor of Alaska (1913–18), and a Canadian to boot. P274-2-6 ALASKA STATE LIBRARY ALASKA GOVERNORS PHOTOGRAPH COLLECTION

headed for the Klondike, where he worked for the *Dawson Daily News* for a short time before moving on to Nome, where he started the *Nome Nugget* on January 1, 1900. From there, he moved to Katalla, then Iditarod, starting newspapers, before establishing the *Alaska Daily Empire* in Juneau. (Incidentally, the *Nugget* and the *Empire* still publish to this day.) Always a community booster, he became active in politics.

In Nome he championed civic improvements including the establishment of a school, a clean water supply and proper waste disposal. He attacked federal incompetence in Alaskan government and railed against Seattle businesses that made fortunes in Alaska but invested little in the north. Strong was very active on behalf of the territory and saw a promising future for Alaskans.

In 1912, he became a member of the Democratic National Convention. The following year, President Woodrow Wilson appointed him governor of Alaska. In a newspaper article at the time, he was described as a native of Kentucky, educated at Brown University. Strong's appointment was a popular choice. According to the *Alaska Daily Empire*, which could hardly be described as unbiased, he was heralded as the unanimous selection of "Democratic clubs, commercial organizations, citizens generally ... miners, fishermen, businessmen and professional men, employers and ... toilers."

One of Strong's achievements was the founding of the Alaska Agricultural College and School of Mines in Fairbanks that later became the University of Alaska. In the 1916 election, Strong supported the Republican James Wickersham for delegate to congress over a Democrat candidate. This angered many hardcore Democrats who vowed to unseat him.

The charge was led by John W. Troy, originally one of Strong's friends and supporters. Troy turned the editorial voice of Strong's former newspaper against him and started calling for his removal from office. In 1917, with Strong's appointment as governor up for renewal, Troy advanced the cause of another Democrat, Thomas Riggs, as Strong's replacement. Strong's opponents tried to discredit him, but he had strong allies in Washington. When that strategy failed, his enemies took another approach common to politics: dig up the dirt.

In early 1918, Troy engaged the Thiel Detective Service Company of St. Louis, Missouri, to look into Strong's past. What they uncovered heralded the end of Strong's political career. They discovered that Strong had been married before, in 1874, and that he had two daughters and a son. Furthermore, the original Mrs. Strong had never sought a divorce nor remarried. J.F.A. Strong was a bigamist!

And that wasn't the worst of it—his detractors discovered something else even more politically devastating. The inner circle of Strong supporters had been aware of his foreign birth, but had assumed that Strong was a naturalized American. James Alexander Strong was actually born in Salmon River, New Brunswick, in 1856; he added the patriotic-sounding middle initial much later.

John Strong was in fact Canadian. Strong's detractors were able to uncover documentation that proved that long after he was assumed to have become an American, he had signed a document that asserted he was still a British subject. That put an end to his political career. He resigned and was replaced by Riggs who completed the remainder of the governor's term. The Strongs left Alaska, spending summers in Seattle and winters in Los Angeles, and travelling extensively around the world.

John and Annie remained together until his death. I could find no evidence that he ever asked for a divorce from his first wife, sought American citizenship or was charged with bigamy. There is nothing that suggests what the second Mrs. Strong thought about all this.

John F.A. Strong died peacefully in Seattle on July 27, 1929, ending the saga of the Canadian who became governor of Alaska.

EXTRAORDINARY
EVENTS

The Colourful World of Early Yukon Politics

Nothing can be more colourful or controversial than politics. When we open the pages of a newspaper they are filled with accounts of scandal and corruption. But few stories illustrate the zealous measures taken by some of those wishing to be elected to high office. In the Yukon, the small population, remoteness, isolation and extremes of weather can make campaigning a real challenge ...

The mob found him a few minutes before 4:00 p.m. hiding in the Fourth Avenue cabin of Montreal Marie, at the north end of Dawson City. He bolted out the back door and sprinted up the hill with a hundred men in hot pursuit. It was early December 1904 and the light was starting to fade. Plumes of vapour from the throats of his pursuers froze in the still winter air as they chased the poor man through the city streets. They finally ran him to the ground, frightened and winded, at Ninth Avenue.

A lynch mob? No—this spirited game of fox and hounds was part of the political scene in the Yukon in 1904. It was federal-election time and in a bid to keep the reins of political power the Liberal government sent Registrar Girouard, keeper of the voters list, into hiding.

The list in his possession contained the names of all the Congdon (Liberal) supporters and none of the Thompson (Conservative) crowd. If this situation was not corrected, Congdon was assured victory in the

The controversy of questionable election practices was captured in this Arthur Buel cartoon during the federal election of 1904. *DAWSON DAILY NEWS*, ARTHUR BUEL CARTOON

imminent election. The same tactic of political evasion took place at Grand Forks, nineteen kilometres from Dawson, where the enumerator waited for direct written instructions before he willingly coughed up the voters list.

Mr. Girouard was reported to have requested asylum from the Mounted Police because of threats on his life. The *Dawson Daily News* sported a front-page cartoon depicting Miss Canada directing two men in suits and bowlers to dig up voters lists that were buried in the ground.

Politics in the Yukon was nothing if not colourful. It was certainly partisan.

One staunch Conservative supporter served the party cause in a heated election by walking 250 kilometres to serve as a scrutineer at the McQuesten Post polling station. In the previous election the Liberals had received more votes there than there were electors. He was rewarded for this act of loyalty with an appointment when the Conservatives won the federal election some years later. This was the nature of politics in the early days of Yukon democracy.

Laura Berton described the mad scramble when the Conservatives won the election of 1911. The Conservative faithful lined up for their promised rewards of jobs from commissioner of the Yukon on down to ditch digger. "Within an hour of the victory the Tories had every possible party member (and some impossible ones)," Berton said, "slated

George Black battled the corrupt Liberal machine, became Commissioner of the Yukon in 1912, and was elected Member of Parliament for the Yukon in 1921.
LIBRARIES AND ARCHIVES CANADA, PHOTO C-039892

for the coveted jobs so long held by the enemy." The employees and supporters of the outgoing government didn't wait to receive their notice; they simply left their desks "without even going through the formality of resigning." The Liberals leaving the Yukon on the stage were practically trampled by the Conservatives now returning in droves to receive their due.

Not all of the not-too-civil servants were as willing to depart. Upon his appointment as commissioner in 1912 and even before his arrival in the Yukon to take over his new responsibilities, George Black announced that government employees could be dismissed on the grounds of incompetence or misconduct including political partisanship. One such government employee sacked by the new commissioner pleaded tearfully to keep his job. Black responded publicly in the newspaper to accusations made against him by stating that the man, T.D. Macfarlane, was notoriously partisan but inefficient as well. Black also scorned the man for his behaviour. He stated in the *Dawson Daily News* of January 31, 1913: "When government officials participate in politics to the extent that many Yukon officials have in the past, they court dismissal on a change of government, and when it comes, they should take their medicine like men, and not blubber about it as did T.D. and D.R. Macfarlane." Fortunately, we can be thankful that such practices have faded away with the passage of time.

While the politics of the period were raucous and partisan, the Yukon campaign trail had its own unique challenges with a riding twice the size of Great Britain. Take, for instance, the 1921 campaign of George Black. The politician was in Vancouver in the fall of that year when a federal election was called. He was nominated to run for the Conservative party against the notorious, if not corrupt, partisan Frederick T. Congdon. He left immediately, travelling by boat up the Alaskan coast to Skagway then by train to Whitehorse. There, due to the river steamers being up on skids for the winter, he carried on overland to the ice-choked Yukon where he paddled to Fort Selkirk in a canoe. I have seen individuals attempt to navigate the October waters of the Yukon many times. Massive blocks of ice swirl in the turbulent river banging together like giant bumper cars at a family fun fair. Anyone braving these conditions in a canoe runs the risk of being crushed or drowned at any moment.

Not willing to waste time waiting at Fort Selkirk until the river froze, Black hired a guide and set out on snowshoe for the silver mines of the Mayo district more than 160 kilometres northeast. When his campaigning in that area was complete, Black travelled by dog team to Dawson City. Somewhere along the trail, he fell through the ice and was drenched. Pushing on, his resistance weakened, he developed a case of pneumonia. I imagine Black fighting his condition while still making speeches in the tiny halls and roadhouses in the Klondike goldfields.

By sheer force of personal effort and determination, he was able to convert certain defeat into a victory over the incumbent Liberal and take a seat in parliament alongside Arthur Meighen and the other members of the official opposition.

But first Black had to make his way to Ottawa. He departed Dawson, travelling via Mayo on his way out of the territory. He had not long left the Klondike capital when the car in which he was driving went off the road and rolled over, pinning him underneath. Fortunately for Black, in those pre-seatbelt days, he suffered only broken ribs and internal injuries, which the wife of an engineer at the North Fork power plant, a trained nurse, tended to until a doctor arrived. After a couple of weeks of enforced rest and recovery, a bed was rigged up for him on a dogsled, and by easy stages he was transported over the winter road to Whitehorse.

Such were the challenges of the north. Through his display of determination and stamina, Black won the respect of the electorate and retained his seat in subsequent elections until he retired nearly thirty years later.

Let's face it—the modern campaigner in the Yukon may well confront physical and logistical challenges greater than those in most other ridings in Canada, but none has been called to exercise the fortitude and endurance shown by George Black in his day.

High Times Continue in the Yukon

I was reading a Canadian joke book when I came across one about the Yukon: "Did you hear that the water system broke down in Dawson City and it was three days before anybody noticed?" Alcohol has had a prominent place in the history of the Yukon, both humorous and not . . .

A micro-distillery in the Yukon? Due to recent changes in legislation, Dorian and Bridget Amos are producing their own brand of vodka in West Dawson. This may be a solid business proposal, or the fodder for another book (Dorian Amos has written two about their Yukon experiences), but there is nothing new in the idea of homemade booze in the far north.

Liquor first entered the Yukon sometime in the 1880s, and its local manufacture soon followed. The earliest European immigrants to the area at that time were veteran prospectors who came in to the interior for the summer looking for gold. They had little room in their packs for large quantities of alcohol. When prospectors and miners started to overwinter, they experienced a life of hardship and deprivation. The earliest of them eked out an existence in summer then hunkered down in crude unheated log cabins to face months of extreme cold and days of darkness. The basic activities of securing food and keeping warm consumed all their energy. Alcohol was not yet a big part of their Yukon experience.

The first record regarding liquor I could find is an article in a Sitka news-paper in 1886 stating that a man named Hawthorne brought fifty gallons of alcohol and liquor into the Yukon "presumably to traffic with the Indians." The following summer a group of Yukon miners celebrated the Fourth of July on their bar claim at the lower end of the Fortymile River by brewing a concoction made of sourdough, hops, oatmeal and a little sugar. This proved quite drinkable. From their supplies, to go along with the homebrew, they improvised a meal of frontier-style baked pork and beans and a boiled plum duff topped with a sauce made from painkiller. In those days, patent medi-cines were liberally spiked with opiates. I imagine the combination must have made for a very good time. Typical in the isolation of the north they

This was a typical saloon in Forty Mile before the Klondike gold rush.
RCMP HISTORICAL COLLECTION, CATALOGUE NUMBER 1934.15.6

had lost track of the actual date. Some late arrivals at their party informed them that the great holiday had passed two days before!

The establishment of the town of Forty Mile was the beginning of many changes for the prospectors. The supply of food and other merchandise became more abundant and diverse. Small comforts, such as decent stoves, became commonplace.

Liquor began to flow into the Yukon valley and the mouths of the men who dotted the countryside. For the first time, there developed a small corps of men who spent their time not looking for gold but instead serving the miners. Saloons became the main focus of Yukon social life, and saloon-keepers the social leaders. Miners who came into the Yukon earlier in the decade, and who later formed the Yukon Order of Pioneers, considered 1888 as the tipping point. After that date, in their eyes, the integrity of newcomers declined. Alcohol played a role in that change.

The saloon was a potent factor in the social shift that was occurring at this time. William Ogilvie described what happened: "There was a big profit in whiskey, and some who were going in, [to the Yukon] anyway, ... took it along and sold it at an enormous advance ... The liquor was sold to the saloon-keepers, who retailed it along with some water at fifty cents a glass.

"Like the saloons everywhere else, they had their clientele of loafers, and, like all the tribe, they interfered with other people's business more than they attended to their own. After the establishment of saloons, miners' meetings were often held in them, and as all present were generally counted miners ... only some were so when they had to be, seeing it was the only means of employment in the country, so all had a vote."

There was also a burgeoning local industry that produced "hootch," the infamous homemade liquor. "Hootch" or "hooch" is American slang for cheap liquor, an expression derived in the late nineteenth century from "Hoochinoo," the Native people of Admiralty Island, south of Juneau, who were distilling their own alcoholic liquor from molasses. They probably learned the process from American traders. The Forty Mile version was made from molasses, dried fruit or berries and fermented with sourdough or hops. Flavoured with anything handy—including old boots and unwashed foot rags—it was aptly named "Forty Rod Whiskey," that being the distance at which it could reputedly kill.

At its peak in the mid-1890s, Forty Mile could boast a theatre, operated by George Snow, one or two dance halls, six saloons and numerous distilleries where hootch was prepared. Bill McPhee and Frank Densmore were soon to open a billiard parlour and saloon to entertain the miners. In 1894, Inspector Constantine of the North-West Mounted Police reported several saloons in operation, selling drinks at fifty cents each. The previous year, three thousand gallons of liquor came into the Yukon.

Hootch production was rife in Forty Mile, and there was a "whiskey gang" that included Jack McQuesten, and T.W. O'Brien. The latter later established the O'Brien Brewery in Dawson City.

Sergeant Brown of the Mounties, who stayed in Forty Mile the winter of 1894, was able to locate nearly all of the thirty-five illicit stills operating in the region. In June 1895, just prior to his departure, he reported, "a lot of drunkenness . . . amongst whites and Indians [in the] spring, but no serious roughs." With the lure of big profits from the Birch Creek diggings downriver in Alaska and the pending arrival of the Mounted Police, many hootchmakers departed for greener pastures in the spring of 1895.

With the arrival of liquor, imported or local, came one of the more infamous practices of the early miners of the Yukon: "the spree." With little else to do during the long winters, many miners came to town for days or weeks of frontier-style drinking that often left them badly hungover and penniless. After their spree, the traders would carry these hapless drinkers on credit for another year of prospecting. Many prospectors were virtually prisoners in the north because of the obligations they had to their provisioners.

Liquor, or lack of it, also led to exciting times. Josiah Spurr, a government geologist conducting a survey of the goldfields in the Yukon basin, experienced this when he stayed with two American customs officers while passing through Circle in 1896. The officers, who had just confiscated two kegs of contraband whiskey, were besieged by "whiskey-dry" miners. They kept the miners at bay only by force of arms. Spurr described a tense night of sentinel duty during which shadowy figures lurked outside the cabin. The booze was stored under his bed.

In the 1940s, the tradition of U-brew was still alive. More than one old-timer told me that the employees of the Yukon Consolidated Gold Corporation, the big dredging company near Dawson City, used to make up a concoction known as "Pruno" in their spare time. It seems miners will go to great lengths to get a buzz. So a change in the liquor laws that has led to this first proposal to manufacture liquor in a small domestic-scale distillery comes as no surprise. It's a tradition that goes back at least 120 years.

It was the "Wets" vs. the "Drys" in the Battle of the Booze

In 1916, the "Wets" and the "Drys" drew a line in the sand over the issue of prohibition.

The word "prohibition" is not part of today's vocabulary. When I was young, prohibition—though dead more than twenty years—was a familiar topic of conversation amongst the adults. You could still see vestiges of this era when I was growing up in Alberta where there were separate entrances to all licensed premises for "Gentlemen" and "Ladies and Escorts." Beer parlours closed from six till seven each evening so that adults could go home and prepare dinner for their children.

I'll distill the controversy of 1916 for you.

The storm surrounding alcohol had been brewing since the turn of the century. The gold rush was an unusual episode in Canadian history when everything was wide open in the Yukon. Gambling, drinking and prostitution were woven into the fabric of the time.

Dawson City, more than Whitehorse, had a reputation as an intoxicating place of wild excess and overindulgence, all under the watchful eye of the Mounted Police. When Dawson City was at its peak, eighty saloons sold liquor day and night.

As the wave of stampeders receded and the population declined, Dawson

Now a historic site, the restored Red Feather Saloon in Dawson City was one of the last to close down. MICHAEL GATES

City took on the veneer of civilization, yet it remained a demographic oddity with a high proportion of highly mobile single men. By 1902, saloon licences had dwindled to ten.

Two decades after the gold rush, Dawson City still had a ratio of drinking establishments per capita ten to fifteen times the national average. By 1911, the population was perhaps two or three thousand, but the town had eighteen licensed hotels, six saloons (one of them now a national historic site) and two wholesale liquor dealers. Alcohol was also being served in the numerous roadhouses in the goldfields. The last two saloons in Dawson City were closed when their licences ran out July 14, 1916. By 1917 the Yukon was the only jurisdiction in Canada outside of Quebec that hadn't banned the sale of booze.

One of the influential books against alcohol was *John Barleycorn*, a classic work written in 1913 by a former Klondike stampeder: Jack London. It accelerated the discontent about booze that was fermenting in society at that time, but the prohibition movement did not emerge as a strong influence until World War I when it became a patriotic duty of Canadians to curb liquor to advance the war effort.

Prohibition became a major issue in the Yukon in 1916. The amount of ink in the newspapers dedicated to the subject is proof of this fact. Prohibition had been championed by the Anglican, Methodist and Presbyterian churches and the Woman's Christian Temperance Union (WCTU), which strove to combat the effects of alcohol on the family.

During the war, The British Empire Club, a patriotic organization formed to support the war effort of Mother England, advocated prohibition as a patriotic act. Then there was the People's Prohibition Movement (PPM), whose 120 Dawson members, some of them the most prominent citizens in the community, voted almost unanimously in favour of banning alcohol. They filled the newspaper with articles condemning liquor and spouting statistics and arguments against the evil liquid.

The economic arguments of the opposing view—that the sale of alcohol was necessary to a healthy economy—was a red herring designed to distract the reader from the main issue of the ruinous effect of booze on society. Naturally, not everyone was a champion of the ban on booze. With Dawson City's unusual demographic makeup, the hotel owners and liquor vendors saw financial disaster coming so they acted to combat the prohibitionists. First, there was the Licensed Victuallers' Association (LVA) who stood to lose a lot of money if the "Prohi's" campaign succeeded. Then another organization formed to combat the prohibition league—the Association of Business Men (ABM) launched their own campaign to counteract the anti-booze movement.

One business that did well out of this debate was the *Dawson Daily News*, which was filled with paid advertising, both pro and con.

Alcohol was ruinous to life and morality, drink wasted manhood, and if booze was banned, people would spend their money on better things, heralded the PPM.

The ABM argued that prohibition would actually ruin the economy of the territory. Fettered by federal control, the territory had few options for revenue generation. Some years, alcohol revenues represented almost 25 percent of the income for the territory. To lose that revenue would be disastrous. Besides, they pointed out, if a man wanted liquor, legal or not, he would find ways to get it. Further, they characterized the prohibitionists as being so-cialists. Women were behind the movement, they suggested, and they didn't contribute to the economy like men did. "Banning alcohol would ruin the economy of the territory," stated their advertisements. Forbidding booze would take away man's right to drink. Real men, they claimed, faced tempta-tion and battled it—take away the choice and you take away manhood. Only a vocal minority, they argued, wanted prohibition. Every argument put forth against booze was contested by the ABM, using their own statistics.

Pressured by both sides, the territorial council resolved to put the issue to a plebiscite on August 30, 1916, letting the sober citizens of the territory have the final say. "Banish the Bar on August 30" became one of the slogans for the "Drys." The vote at the end of August was hardly decisive: the "Wets" won the day by a mere three votes—874 to 871. Ninety percent of eligible electors had turned out to cast their ballot. The potential loss of liquor rev-enue was probably the deciding factor. Two years later, it became a moot issue when the federal government placed a wartime ban on the manufac-ture, transportation and sale of alcohol. Liquor licences in the territory were terminated. Ottawa offset the potentially devastating loss of revenue with an additional subsidy.

At the conclusion of the war, the ban on liquor was lifted, but two years later in 1920 another plebiscite on the issue went in favour of the "Drys." Prohibition lasted less than a year. When Ottawa reduced the subsidies to the territory, the electors quickly voted to reinstate the sale of alcohol to boost the Yukon's public budget. This time, the sale of liquor was through government outlets. Saloons had disappeared, and hotels were permitted only the sale of beer. This ultimately gave rise to the infamous "snake rooms" in the hotels of the 1920s to '40s . . . but that's another story.

Christmas a Special Celebration in the Yukon

The Yukon is a special place. You can get an enhanced sense of this by celebrating Christmas here. I remember one Christmas Eve in Dawson City when the all-important mail truck with its load of gifts was behind schedule. It was far too late in the day to sort mail when it finally arrived, nevertheless the staff stayed through the evening to ensure everybody received their vital packages. I also recall that Dawsonites, realizing the postal workers were sacrificing their own time to get the mail delivered, brought in food and other goodies to show gratitude. It was one of the finest Christmas experiences that I recollect, yet it pales in comparison to the Yukon's earlier Christmas celebrations...

It was 1894 and Emilie Tremblay couldn't have chosen a more unlikely place to celebrate Christmas. Her new home—a one-room sod-roof cabin with a single window—was located on her husband's mining claim on Miller Creek in the Sixtymile district, ninety kilometres west of the future site of Dawson City. Previously, it had been occupied by her husband, Jack, and his partners.

Already several years old, the cabin had a dirt floor partially covered with wood. Along the walls were the primitive bunks on which the miners slept. A single pole in the centre of the cabin supported the roof. At the foot of this post was a thick black layer of spit. The men, tired from working on their claim all day, lay in their bunks chewing tobacco and spitting at the pole.

Tobacco chewing was an indulgence practised throughout the Yukon. As one man said: "It is impossible to keep anything clean. Nothing is sacred to him . . . If a miner happens to have a clean stove about the place, and a man drops in with his cud in his mouth, the first thing he invariably does is to spit on the stove. It is a sort of recognized salutation—an informal way of starting conversation!"

Emilie Tremblay took a shovel and started her cleanup at the centre of this room, and in the following days scoured her new home from top to bottom. The cabin was equipped with the barest of essentials and crudely built furniture.

She was one of the first white women to come over the Chilkoot Pass into the interior of the Yukon. Among the thousand prospectors in the Yukon River drainage area at that time, there may have been two dozen other white women scattered along the Yukon valley. Emilie was the only woman living on this Sixtymile tributary. When they came to the north, women faced extreme conditions unlike anything that they had been prepared for. Many early chroniclers spoke with admiration of these women; and, overall they were treated with considerable respect.

Emilie Fortin was born in Quebec and later moved to New York State. It was there, in 1893 that she met and married Pierre Nolasque (Jack) Tremblay, a Miller Creek miner who had come Outside that summer to visit his family in the east. The following spring, the newlyweds departed for the Yukon, crossing the Chilkoot Pass early in the season and arriving in Fortymile on June 16. After organizing their affairs in Fortymile, they made the twenty-mile journey upriver and walked over the hills to Jack's claim on Miller Creek.

For Emilie Tremblay, it was a difficult adjustment. The miners felt the creek was no place for the fairer sex. There were no other women and she was further isolated by the fact that she did not speak English.

Upon her arrival, Emilie immediately started working on her grammar and vocabulary. Her English gradually improved, and by the following spring she was joined on Miller Creek by the French-Canadian wife of one of the Day brothers, a woman she had met the previous spring in Juneau.

Being the only woman on the creek at that time, though, she decided that she and Jack should offer a Christmas dinner to the miners living nearby. This proved a challenge as there were none of the usual amenities to help make Christmas dinner a success.

They improvised, writing invitations on birch bark. The guests were asked to bring their own utensils to eat their meal. Preparations were further complicated by the fact that she could only cook dishes small enough to fit into their tiny twenty-two-inch oven. She had little with which to cheer up and civilize her primitive log home so she adapted an unused long skirt to serve as a tablecloth. The Christmas menu was a selection of stuffed rabbit, roast caribou and brown beans in broth. There were King Oscar sardines, evaporated potatoes, and sourdough bread with butter, as well as cake and a plum pudding with blueberry sauce for dessert.

Just before the end of the meal, a latecomer arrived with a bottle of rum to add to the festivities. He had walked all the way to Fortymile and back in the bitter winter weather to obtain the liquor. After the meal, they played cards and filled the cabin with tobacco smoke and good cheer.

In later years, Emilie reflected on the first year she spent on Miller Creek;

Emilie Tremblay was one of the first white women to celebrate Christmas in the Yukon. A school in Whitehorse is now named in her honour. VEAZZIE WILSON PHOTO, AUTHOR'S COLLECTION

she regarded that and the improvised Christmas celebrated with the good-hearted miners as the best time she ever had.

In the following spring of 1895, she planted a garden on the roof of her cabin to improve their diet. By the end of the summer, the Tremblays had mined enough gold to facilitate a return to New York State, but they couldn't get the north out of their blood. They soon returned to the Yukon to live out their days in the Klondike. Madame Tremblay eventually established a dry-goods store in Dawson City, which she operated for many years. She became a highly respected member of the community, and today a school in Whitehorse is named in her honour.

Over the years, Yukoners have also found many ways in which to improvise their celebrations of Christmas in the isolation, cold and dark. I remember with some amusement the comments of a newly arrived work colleague, who had just experienced his first Christmas in Dawson City. Being a rather proper Englishman and a High Anglican, he was nonplussed by his experience at the inter-denominational Christmas Eve service traditionally celebrated in St. Paul's Anglican Church. The minister, he reported, was wearing mukluks instead of proper footwear. There were dogs wandering about in the church during the service, and the improvised heating system—that for years had failed to provide adequate heat for the typically frigid service—had to be augmented prior to the beginning of the ceremony by kerosene-fired heaters that roared like jet engines. Sitting at the back of the church in the rapidly declining temperatures, the air filled with fumes, one shivering parishioner loudly urged the minister to hurry up and finish the service so that they could all go home and warm up! Never in all his years had my friend experienced anything like that Christmas Eve service in Dawson City!

Beyond the pomp and ceremony that the yuletide season can bring, beyond the abundance our affluent society enjoys, there is something essential about a Yukon Christmas. Neither formality nor gifts are required—simply the spirit of the occasion and the joyful sharing of a community coming together at the coldest, darkest time of year.

The Little School that Saved the Yukon

Never underestimate the influence a few schoolchildren can have on the course of major political issues . . .

As a result of fifteen Catholic students back in 1937, the Yukon Territory was spared annexation to the province of British Columbia.

To understand the origin of this episode in Yukon history we must rewind to July of 1899 when William Ogilvie, Commissioner of the Yukon—having disposed of numerous pressing matters in the running of a newly formed territory—got around to the issue of education. He met with representatives of the Anglican, Catholic, Methodist and Presbyterian churches. While the three Protestant clergymen agreed that a non-sectarian public school be established, the Catholic representative, Father Pierre Gendreau, disagreed. His reason for dissent could be followed back to education and minority rights issues in Manitoba. Father Gendreau requested that a separate school be established, funded by taxes from supporters and a government grant. It was to be staffed by the Sisters of St. Ann in a building already constructed.

The government was desperate for a school, and when the ship containing the supplies for a public school sank, the territorial council was willing to support anybody who could start one. On September 3, 1899, St. Mary's Catholic School was opened for thirty-seven students. It was inspected and financial support was put in place, making it Dawson City's first publicly supported institution of learning.

While this was intended to be a temporary measure, by 1901 council had approved an ordinance that ensured support of both public and separate schools. This was further reinforced a year later when council agreed to a more substantial ordinance governing schools, even though at the time seven of the ten councillors were Protestant. Approval was given with little controversy. The Sisters of St. Ann ran a good school at low cost to the government, and provided education to a significant number of the population—fluctuating between seven to forty percent of the school-aged children of Dawson City.

On two early occasions, once in 1905 and again in 1912, the question of annexation by British Columbia arose. The first time, Liberal and Conservative politicians in BC raised the objection that recognition of separate schools in their province would lead to sectarian conflict. The issue emerged again when Manitoba, then much smaller than today, attempted to enlarge its jurisdiction all the way north to Hudson Bay. Territorial-council members raised the issue of supporting separate schools in the Yukon. The question was referred to Ottawa, and bolstered by Prime Minister Borden's adamant desire to avoid "another Manitoba schools question" the commissioner was able to fend off proponents of annexation.

The most serious threat came many years later and sprang from the dreams of a former Klondiker who had risen to become the premier of British Columbia: Thomas Dufferin "Duff" Pattullo.

The Pattullo family was politically connected to the Liberal government in Ottawa. When Klondike fever swept the continent he was able to obtain the position of principal secretary to Yukon's first commissioner, James Walsh. Pattullo accompanied the commissioner's entourage of civil servants to the Yukon, where he witnessed first-hand the corruption of the Walsh administration. When later appointed as acting Gold Commissioner he worked long and hard to clean up the tarnished image of the mining recorder's office, even receiving praise from the press for his accomplishments.

Pattullo left his job with the government in 1901 and was quickly immersed in Liberal party politics in Dawson. He became appalled by and a strong opponent of the corrupt political machine operated by Frederick

T. Congdon. Because of this, Pattullo and many others in a divided Yukon Liberal camp supported Conservative candidate Alfred Thompson in the federal election of 1904.

Pattullo moved to Prince Rupert, where he again became involved in politics, eventually becoming premier of British Columbia in November of 1933. Duff never forgot his connection to the Yukon, and saw the natural resources of the north as a way out of the depression that gripped the country through most of the 1930s. Annexation, he thought, would ensure the construction of the Alaska Highway and pro-

The students who attended this school in the 1930s were responsible for preventing the annexation of the Yukon by the province of British Columbia.
MICHAEL GATES

vide access to resources that would lead the way out of the stagnant economy. Gold had nearly doubled in price and mining held the promise of prosperity.

The constitutional fate of the Yukon and its tiny population lay in the hands of the federal government, which during the 1930s had viewed the territory as a financial liability. If British Columbia were to take this liability off their hands, it would reduce the federal deficit, so Prime Minister Mackenzie King was receptive to the possibility.

Late in 1936, the two governments began negotiating the terms for a transfer and agreed to a number of conditions for it to proceed in April of 1937. Pattullo made it part of his campaign for re-election in 1937; winning the election would be seen as an endorsement of the annexation. The Yukon council voiced objections but the tiny population of the territory was viewed to be inconsequential by Ottawa. Pattullo boldly announced the pending signing of a tentative transfer agreement for October 2, 1937.

Pattullo's enthusiasm and optimism had blinded him to the one factor that would bring his plan to a halt. If the Yukon was to be annexed, it would mean violating certain minority rights to education that had existed in the territory for four decades, or introducing a separate school system in British Columbia.

The spectre of annexation finally brought forward objections in British Columbia by the Protestant Orange Order and the Vancouver Ministerial Association. The Catholic minority, on the other hand, responded positively to the idea of separate schools for the province. Once the issue was exposed to the public, though, both the federal and provincial governments completely lost interest in annexation.

Where the budgetary interests of the federal government would be advanced, the objections of the tiny population of the Yukon were ignored along with the protests of the provincial opposition. Likewise, the issues of rewriting the boundaries were shrugged off, and the provincial election seemed ready to give Pattullo his mandate.

But the presence of a small Catholic school consisting then of just fifteen students in the isolated town of Dawson City sent Pattullo's dream crashing to an end. No one wanted the ship of state to founder on the rocky reef of minority rights, a federal issue that conflicted with the provinces' ability to determine their own educational policy.

I, for one, am glad that's how it worked out. More power to the children.

Terrorism in the Klondike

Remember 9/11? Yes, we all do. We can all instantly bring to mind precisely where we were and what we were doing the moment we became aware of the terrorist attack. I was in Vancouver staying with friends before catching a flight back to Whitehorse when I woke up to the televised horror of the World Trade Center collapsing.

After my initial shock, followed by frustration over the cancellation of all flights and an ensuing three-hour wait on the telephone while trying to reach a booking agent at Air Canada, I realized life was nevertheless going on pretty much as usual in Vancouver. Not so in Whitehorse where everyone was paralyzed by panic and confusion as two potentially hijacked jumbo jets were forced to land there because America wouldn't have them. My wife and daughter experienced this and I wasn't there to support them.

The Yukon has a history stained with terrorism and plotting . . .

An act of terrorism was not a total surprise in New York. There had been previous attempts to destroy the World Trade Center. Back in 1920, suspected Italian terrorists used forty-five kilograms of dynamite to blow up a horse and cart on Wall Street, killing thirty-nine people. The papers were filled with news about the event and the attorney general called for tougher laws and an increased budget to combat terrorism. Sounds familiar, doesn't it?

Thankfully, the Yukon experience with 9/11 turned out to be a false alarm resulting from panic and miscommunication: the jets were filled only with frightened and bewildered tourists and in the end there was not one terrorist in the lot. Nevertheless, before this agonizing day the Yukon too had not been exempt from the tension and intrigue of terrorism; you only have to look into the past.

By the 1880s, the British and Americans had agreed on a dividing line that would separate Canada from the United States. But in those early days of the Yukon nobody knew just where it was to be drawn. The Yukon River basin started filling up with prospectors, most from the United States. For a while, the US had a post office on Canadian soil mainly because there was a question as to the whereabouts of the dividing line. That changed in 1887 when Canadian surveyor William Ogilvie located the point where the boundary crossed the Yukon River. A few years later, he came back to the Yukon and extended the line southward, thus confirming that the Sixtymile goldfields were located in Canada.

Many American prospectors retreated to the American side of the border when the Mounties arrived. Because of this, Alaskan governor James Shakely wrote the US secretary of war asking for soldiers to maintain order in American territory. Many feared the presence of the Mounted Police on the Canadian side would force the seedier individuals over the border.

There was continuing unease between Britain and the United States over the territory until the boundary was established. Every once in a while the newspapers would stir up patriotic feelings over the issue. During the gold rush, the North-West Mounted Police established posts at the summit of the passes leading into the interior. These points were where the boundary was eventually established, leaving Yukoners without access to a saltwater port and depriving Americans of territory in the interior.

This arrangement was not satisfactory to some and led to Yukon's first episode of intrigue and conspiracy. In the spring of 1901, Superintendent Primrose, in charge of the Mounted Police in Dawson, heard rumours that a band of Americans in Skagway were plotting to seize the Yukon from Canada by force. A group of Alaskans planned to invade Canada from Skagway,

Circle and Eagle, downriver from Dawson City. The group behind the conspiracy was called the Order of the Midnight Sun. The Mounties responded by sending an undercover agent to Seattle and an officer to Skagway. At higher levels, Canada did receive some co-operation from the US government. In addition, Clifford Sifton, Canada's minister of the interior, decided to beef up the Whitehorse district by fifty officers so that the number of men posted to the Dalton Trail could be doubled and the number of men at Whitehorse increased to one hundred. Time passed and nothing happened. By the end of 1901, the supposed plot to capture the Yukon was defused and the event slipped into the history books as nothing more than an interesting sidebar. Nevertheless, shortly after this peaceful finale, an article in the *Seattle Daily Times* exposed details of the conspiracy—including plans to cut telegraph lines, capture the Mounted Police detachments and create a "Klondike Free State." If the Mounties hadn't taken a serious interest in the threat of attack, would things have turned out differently?

Yet another incident of terrorism in the Yukon occurred February 21,

The Klondike was subject to a terrorist attack when an anarchist bombed this gold-mining dredge in 1913. LIBRARIES AND ARCHIVES CANADA, PHOTO PA 103862

1913, when the Yukon Gold Company Dredge Number 1 was dynamited. The explosives had been stolen from Yukon Gold's own nearby powder house. Armed guards were posted near the other dredges, and a $5,000 reward was offered.

A threatening letter was sent to the company warning them not to pursue the case any further. During the investigation, ski tracks were discovered in the vicinity of the damaged dredge and since cross-country skiing was uncommon at that time, suspicion fell upon a group of Swedes. One had been seen in the vicinity of some of the dredges earlier in the season. The efforts of the police to gather evidence against the main suspect, a Scandinavian known as "The Educated Swede," proved fruitless. His account that he had heard the explosion and skied out to investigate seemed plausible. There was so little crime in Dawson City that the Mounties were a little rusty with their investigative skills.

Here's where the story gets interesting.

The Yukon Gold Company became impatient, so R.E. Franklin, their electrical superintendent, planted a primitive electronic eavesdropping device in the Swedes' cabin. While the Swedes discussed the matter inside the cabin, laughing at the stupidity of the police and mining company, Franklin crouched outside in the dark with his notebook, copying down their confessions. One member of the group, actually a Norwegian named Jacob Nielson, was arrested and convicted of the bombing by a six-man jury. He was sentenced to twenty years in prison. A combination of socialist ideas and a case of cabin fever had combined to create this act of violence.

Yet, despite the episodes of terrorism in its past, the Yukon—remote, immense and sparsely populated—remains an unlikely target for terrorist attack. Should we rest easy with this knowledge?

"Languorous Lilies of Soulless Love"

They have been called "soiled doves," "ladies of easy virtue," "fair but frail," and, yes, "languorous lilies of soulless love." They have been reviled as a stain on society, and they have been glamorized in western lore. Whatever way you look at it, prostitution has had a colourful history in the Yukon.

As soon as miners started arriving in the Yukon, women followed to meet the demand for affection. The first fallen woman to enter the Yukon is believed to have been "Dutch" Kate, who accompanied a group of prospectors over the Chilkoot in 1888, a full ten years before the gold rush. Once the town of Forty Mile was established, a troupe of entertainers arrived on the scene. The women among the ensemble were amply rewarded for the "display of their talents." One of them was known as "The Virgin" because, it was alleged, she had once seen one.

The advent of the gold rush brought with it the development of a red-light district in Dawson City known as Paradise Alley and located behind Front Street. Most of these women worked independently, but Mattie Silks, a successful madam from Denver, braved the Chilkoot Trail in early 1898 with eight working girls. Mattie set up shop in a two-storey house on Second Avenue, where she operated for three months. During that time, her girls earned thirty to fifty dollars a day. Factoring in inflation, that works out to

Prostitution was accepted as part of life in Dawson during the Klondike gold rush. YUKON ARCHIVES, VANCOUVER PUBLIC LIBRARY FONDS, PHOTO #02074

roughly seventy-two thousand dollars in today's currency—and that doesn't include tips! After accounting for overhead expenses and covering the gambling debt amassed by her husband, Mattie netted thirty-eight thousand dollars, equivalent to almost a million dollars in modern-day cash. Not bad for three months' work!

Prostitution extended out into the goldfields as well. Grand Forks, the largest of the outlying communities, had its own red-light district at the far end of First Avenue, a short distance from the Mounted Police detachment. Other creek communities had their own districts that varied in size.

With the gold cleanup in the spring, there was always an abundance of gold dust out on the creeks. On the Queen's birthday in 1899, a well-known businessman brought eleven prostitutes over King Solomon Dome on pack horses to a roadhouse near Upper Discovery on Dominion Creek, about sixty-five kilometres from Dawson. That night $4,000 was taken in at the bar. Festivities continued during the next day and night. One girl alone carried $500 worth of Dominion Creek Gold back to Dawson.

Business petered out very quickly in the goldfields as the more profitable ground was exhausted, but some women continued to ply their trade long after the stampede had faded. One, a notorious member of the demi-monde named Gypsy Troll, operated first at Sulphur Creek and then later at Granville and Gold Run. Laura Berton reported that Gypsy had been involved in a stabbing a few days prior to a visit the author made to Granville sometime around 1908.

Prostitutes bore a stigma that repelled the respectable women of Dawson. On the streets they were shunned, and shops were only open to them during specific hours.

Yet, for all of the tawdry associations these women shouldered, they also fascinated the upright citizens of the community. In *I Married the Klondike*, Laura Berton—mother of well-known Canadian author Pierre Berton—alludes to her voyeuristic walks beyond Lousetown, from where she and her walking companion could spy on the "ladies of the line" relaxing in the off-hours of the afternoon. Lousetown, or Klondike City, was located at the mouth of the Klondike River on the opposite shore from Dawson, and well separated from the conventional mores of the Klondike capital.

Betty Neumiller, who lived in Dawson just after the turn of the twentieth century, remembered being driven by curiosity as a child to visit these

Now a restored hotel, Bombay Peggy's, in Dawson City, was reputed to have been a brothel for a short period of time. MICHAEL GATES

Ruby's Place, now designated as nationally significant, was a house of prostitution for many years.
MICHAEL GATES

exotic ladies, one of whom offered her and her friend a small orange each. Oranges were a rarity and special treat in Dawson in those times. Another woman even gave her a small ring to wear, but in embarrassment, Betty threw it into the Klondike River from the bridge on her way home, fearing her parents would learn of the forbidden visit across the river.

By the 1930s, prostitutes had become an accepted part of the community. Unlike members of the profession Outside, the local practitioners were respected and trusted. Some provided banking services, while others reliably held money for miners who occasionally visited town. Many were able to leave with a bankroll to establish successful and legitimate businesses in the south while others married well and achieved social acceptance in the process.

Ruby Scott, the most famous post-gold rush madam in the Yukon, enjoyed a high level of respect in Dawson City, and was known for her generosity and love of children. Dances were often held in the Oddfellow's Hall (now restored as the Odd Gallery and art school in Dawson). During breaks in the music, men would bring their dates next door to Ruby's to escape the liquor restrictions of the day. There, Ruby would offer drinks and conversation to her guests. In time Ruby received one of the highest forms of acceptance any community can bestow. Her former home and base of operation was designated as nationally significant by the Historic Sites and Monuments Board of Canada, and is now cared for by Parks Canada.

Prostitution has, in fact, become downright quaint in its historic context. Bombay Peggy's, known for its brief history as a brothel and since refurbished into a modern-day hotel, now provides a colourful setting for guests who patronize its rooms. Historic walking tours in Dawson City would not be complete without a passing reference to Paradise Alley and a stop at Ruby's Place. It is a popular spot for tourists, who have on occasion asked me to take their photograph standing on the steps of the former brothel. I often see husbands handing cameras to their wives here and asking them to take a picture.

Prostitution has slipped into the misty realm of myth and achieved iconic status in the territory, being further twisted and distorted by its spurious association with cancan dancing. In 1992, then editor of the *Yukon News* Peter Lesniak was lambasted by members of the community for editorial comments he made about disbanding a local group of cancan dancers, whom he described as "thick-thighed hoofers."

"As we all know," he said, "cancan dancers doubled as whores during the Klondike Gold Rush." Protesters proceeded to picket the *News* and wrote letters to the editor claiming his remarks undermined Yukon's heritage.

Of course, cancan dancers did not exist in the Yukon's early days, so there could not have been any link to prostitution. But why let that get in the way of a good story?

HISTORY, HISTORY EVERYWHERE

History Revealed in Old Tin Cans

In the Yukon we have a territorial bird, a territorial flower and a territorial tree. I would like to nominate a territorial artifact: the tin can . . .

After scouring the landscape of the Yukon for several decades I have learned one thing: old tin cans are everywhere. You may find just a single one with its lid pried open lying on a hilltop overlooking one of the Yukon's countless magnificent vistas, or you may find them piled by the hundreds at old cabin sites.

I once came across an abandoned temporary sawmill site that dated to the construction of the Alaska Highway. Piled behind it were so many rusting beer cans I had to wonder how the operators managed to cut a straight piece of wood. A pile of castaway tins is a sure sign that somebody lived nearby. While conducting a survey of historical remains on Black Hills Creek near the Stewart River more than twenty-five years ago, I found that while many sites had been stripped of picks, shovels, lanterns and other saleable antiques, the rusty tins were always left behind. The collectors had overlooked some of the greatest treasures of all.

During the gold rush, every immigrant was required to bring in a ton of supplies. For preservation and ease of handling the food was usually in tin cans: tins of corned beef, stewed tomatoes, sardines, soup and—most important of all—beans. Many five-gallon fuel tins made their way into the north as well. The tin can was the universal container; cast off upon being opened and never given a second glance—or so I thought.

The fact is, without the tin can, life in the north would have been much less liveable.

What makes the tin can so useful in this regard is its physical character. Tin cans are malleable and can be bent or shaped easily. They can be cut, riveted, nailed and screwed, soldered, drilled, punched, folded, rolled, flattened and scribed with ease. In their abandoned condition, these cans had not lost their utility. As I came to learn, these containers were only just beginning to be useful. They were in fact the object of the ultimate northern makeover.

The first reused tin can I recognized was resting on a shaky and weathered wooden table in the exposed interior of a long-abandoned log cabin. It was an old tobacco tin with the lid screwed tight. Inserted in a hole gouged in the lid was the burnt-down remnant of a candle. Recovered from the garbage heap, this tin can had taken on a new life as a candle holder. I began to look more closely at the tins I had for so long ignored. Everywhere, there were examples of cans reused for one purpose or another. I have found more than sixty different uses so far, and the list keeps growing.

Cut out the top off a five-gallon kerosene can and run some haywire across the opening, and you have an instant bucket. I have seen these depicted in numerous historical photographs from the Yukon Archives. Take the same can and open one of the long sides and you have a container for feeding dogs or something to catch crankcase oil.

Another popular adaptation was lighting devices. Hanging in nearly every abandoned cabin I have found a variety of tin cans modified for candles. My Parks Canada colleague Christine Hedgecock let me use a candle holder on the Chilkoot Trail that she had fashioned from an empty can of olive oil. It was cut open on the top and one side, and the shiny interior reflected the candle flame and cast a respectable light.

The old-timers know these candle lanterns on sight. They even have a name for them: "bugs." Easy to fashion with the simplest of tools from the ever-present raw material, they worked well and, because the enclosed candle was protected from vagrant breezes, didn't easily blow out.

Some of the other wonderful creations I have seen include portable stoves, berry pickers, moose callers, ashtrays, a mailbox, cribbage boards and a foot-powered lapidary set-up. I have seen watering cans, honey buckets and a device that would keep toilet paper dry. And, yes, they even make a better mousetrap.

I doubt the old cabins in the territory would have been liveable without the ubiquitous kerosene can. They were used as wall and roof coverings, chimney caps and stove-pipe safeties. Placed on the wall behind or the floor beneath a stove, they protected homes from catching on fire and, wrapped around the legs of the family cache, helped to keep rodents out. And these beautiful cre-

A typical miner's tin candle lamp, or "bug," found in the Klondike goldfields. MICHAEL GATES

ations in all their unique applications and individual design tell us a lot about Yukon life in the first half of the twentieth century.

The Yukon is a big land with few people. In the early days, trails and crude wagon roads facilitated travel. The rivers were the highways of that time. Transportation was costly, and people didn't move around as easily as they do now. Many lived isolated lives and seldom came to town. They learned to make do, so it isn't a surprise that when someone needed something they didn't have, it was easier and cheaper to turn to the pile of cast-off tin cans and fashion something than it was to walk to town to make a purchase.

Out of interest I have looked to other parts of the world to see if the same reuse of tin cans is practised elsewhere. I have seen examples from third-world countries where interesting curiosities were fabricated from other people's cast-offs and sold to tourists. In Cuba where material goods are often in short supply because of the American embargo, many items are made over. In upstate New York I saw examples of obsolete farming equipment being converted into ornaments to decorate yards along rural roads. But never have I seen as many examples of utilitarian reuse as are found in the north.

There seem to be three factors that influence the practice of reuse. First, there is means: the physical properties of the tin can lend themselves to easy altering and reshaping. Second, there is opportunity. In the Yukon the universal availability of the tin can meant that they were close at hand whenever the need arose for something. Third, there was the motivation. Isolation breeds ingenuity. In the north, especially a hundred years ago, this was very much the case. In an era when miners didn't go to town for years at a stretch, when something was needed the fabricator couldn't wait for a trip to the hardware store.

This tradition of reuse hasn't died out, although today it has changed form and material. A visit to a modern home or camp reveals that the plastic container has primarily replaced the tin can. But while our modern plastics are certainly reusable and also recyclable, in my eyes they will never have the malleability, usefulness or the beauty of the classic tin can.

There's Film in Them Thar Hills

The Dawson Film Find was one of the many unique experiences I enjoyed during my career with Parks Canada. At the time, I had no idea of the crazy reaction that would come from the public—or of the hype it would generate.

Sometimes, the strangest things can happen. They aren't planned or expected, but they leave a lasting impact.

I had just started working for Parks Canada as curator of their massive artifact collection in Dawson City back in 1978. It was the beginning of my first summer in the Klondike and there was already plenty to do when David Burley, a Parks Canada archeologist, suggested I take a look at what had been uncovered in the empty lot behind Diamond Tooth Gertie's. At one time, the three-storey Dawson Amateur Athletic Association (DAAA) building stood there complete with swimming pool (summer) and hockey arena (winter).

As construction began on a new hockey rink, a city crew had uncovered some noteworthy debris: chicken wire, broken curling rocks, bottles, metal canisters and numerous reels of old film. The film was later determined to be the old highly flammable nitrate-based variety. Discoveries like these were not uncommon in Dawson City. Virtually every construction job, road restoration or foundation repair exposed a treasure trove from the gold-rush days.

The old films still contained the images that were once projected onto the screens of Dawson City's theatres. By chance, I found an advertisement in an old issue of the *Dawson Daily News* for one of the reels that I had just examined stating that it was to be shown in Dawson City in the fall of 1917. This piqued my curiosity.

I started to phone contacts I had in Ottawa and Montreal to see if there was any interest in this discovery. There wasn't—at least, until I spoke to Sam Kula, director of the National Film Archives in Ottawa. The next thing I knew, Sam was on his way to Dawson City.

Sam Kula (l.) and the author examine some of the film salvaged from the permafrost in Dawson City, 1978. KATHY JONES-GATES

Hollywood had lost a big chunk of its early film history when warehouses containing the highly flammable nitrate silent-movie films burned to the ground. Sam thought it would be worth looking at these old movies to see if they contained any lost work of the silent-film era.

On the excavation site at Fifth Avenue and Queen Street, Kathy Jones, director of the Dawson City Museum, and Sam and I plotted out a plan to recover and identify as many of these films as possible. The discovery was to be known as the Dawson Film Find. That summer hundreds of reels of highly flammable film were salvaged and identified. Workers were stationed in what we determined to be the safest place to do such work: the old acetylene plant at Bear Creek, nine kilometres from Dawson City. The building had metal-lined walls and cement floors.

We eventually learned how the film came to be buried in the ground. In a letter to the community newsletter the *Klondike Korner*, Clifford Thomson, a retired banker, described how fifty years earlier he had the film taken from the basement of the Carnegie Library on Queen Street and carted down the road to the Dawson Amateur Athletic Association building. There it was thrown into the no longer useable swimming pool.

This wasn't the work my boss had in mind for me so I found myself slipping out to Bear Creek at the end of the day to see how the museum crew was progressing. None of the recovered footage contained anything to do with the Klondike, or even the Yukon, for that matter. It consisted of Hollywood films of all types: comedies, westerns, serials and romances. Some of the most famous names in Hollywood were featured. Also contained in the unearthed treasure were almost two hundred reels of news footage of the day. Many had Canadian content and therefore were of considerable interest to the National Film Archives.

When the first list of titles reached Ottawa their public-relations department went into high gear. The next thing we knew, newspapers from all over the world were announcing the discovery. The Dawson City Museum and Parks Canada were swamped with telephone inquiries from every corner of the planet.

Back in Ottawa, Kula was gearing up for the restoration of the flammable but extremely valuable footage. Special equipment was required to copy the reels frame by frame. The photo-processing equipment became clogged with rust particles and the work was painstakingly slow. He contacted the US Library of Congress and they too got into the act. While Ottawa was interested in the Canadian newsreels, Washington was keen to retrieve the Hollywood content.

But first, we had to find a way to get the film to Ottawa. Storing the material in the Yukon was not an option because of its instability, but nobody would agree to transport the tonne of films, classified as hazardous. We managed to get them to Whitehorse but any attempt to put them onto a bus, plane or moving van was refused by the local firms. The Dawson Film Find had become notorious and everyone in the territory seemed to know what was going on. Fortunately, we were able to arrange for the armed forces, who frequently work with explosives, to fly the crates of film to Rockcliffe Airforce Base in our nation's capital.

A year later, Dawson City was recovering from a devastating flood. Despite that—and amidst great fanfare—the first showing of the restored silent movies was made to an enthusiastic full house in Dawson's Palace Grand Theatre in early September 1979. Fred Bass, a retired pianist from Vancouver who had started his career playing in silent-movie theatres, provided accompaniment. The show was a success and helped lift community spirits after a trying summer.

To this day, more than thirty years after the discovery, I still get inquiries about the Dawson Film Find. It has been featured in documentaries, including an ambitious documentary titled *Popcorn with Maple Syrup*, and the subject of a multitude of magazine and newspaper articles. In 2004, a number of the films that were salvaged and restored were featured at the Dawson City International Short Film Festival.

Many times during my years of working in Dawson City, I've heard stories of how loads of gold-rush artifacts dug up or discovered in the old buildings were taken down to the waterfront and thrown into the river. This was one time that we managed to save a legacy. If I had followed all of the government directives and policies on health and safety or simply stuck to my job description, the Dawson Film Find would have never happened. Being young and enthusiastic—and perhaps just a little foolish—I followed it through with satisfying results.

Others received recognition for their part in the discovery. Alderman

Frank Barrett was presented with the Commissioner's Award for having the foresight to stop a municipal crew from excavating the material and throwing it away. Kathy Jones was recipient of the Yukoner Award from the Yukon Visitors Association, the predecessor of today's Tourism Industry Association of the Yukon (TIA Yukon), for her role in publicizing the event and bringing recognition to the Yukon. And I received the best award of all. A little over a year after the whole thing started, Kathy and I were married—and we still are to this day!

The Cabin on Gold Run Claim Number 24

"Empty cabins, haunting ghosts, loved the life that could not last,
Tattered curtains on the windows of the memories of the past."
—*from the song "Tattered Curtains" by Lana Rae*

Old things often evoke strong feelings of a lyric past, in the way an old cabin sparked award-winning Yukon musician Lana Rae to write a song about her personal encounter with history.

I had a similar experience many years ago when, as part of my work, I sighted some interesting things from a helicopter flying over the Klondike goldfields. They consisted of derelict buildings, old mine workings, gravel tailings and a scattered array of old boilers and abandoned steam machines. To get a closer look, my wife, Kathy, and I took a Sunday drive up an overgrown road to Gold Run Creek, a tributary of Dominion Creek near the abandoned community of Granville, one hundred kilometres south of Dawson City.

Little was known about this creek when we first travelled there back then in 1982. Certainly, it didn't conjure up the tangible reminders of the gold rush as did Eldorado and Bonanza creeks. In fact, there wasn't much left but a few rusting boilers scattered about and rotting cabins with tattered curtains hanging limply in the windows. People had lived there, but who were they and what were their lives like?

The old abandoned cabin on Gold Run Creek, 1982. MICHAEL GATES

It was Kathy who saw the first cabin. When she brought it to my attention, I stopped the truck and climbed out to investigate. All that could be seen was the tin roof, jutting above the willow underbrush. I clambered up the bank and through roadside vegetation to get a better look. I didn't know then that this chance encounter would lead me to years of discovery on this tiny, obscure tributary. There before me lay the remains of an old mining claim and on it the tattered remnants of someone's life.

Motivated to discover and examine more of these sites, I applied for and received a small grant from the Canada Council to investigate the abandoned relics in the Klondike goldfields. With Yukon photographer and friend Richard Hartmier, I hurried to record the remains before they became victim to the renewed mining activity of the early '80s. We travelled all over the goldfields taking pictures, talking to local residents and gathering a small selection of artifacts for the Dawson Museum.

But for some visceral reason this site drew me back many times. I sought answers from the remains. Using my archeological background to guide me I carefully photographed and recorded all of the artifacts: a small log cabin with an outhouse nearby, a woodpile, a collapsed shed and a second smaller log structure with a large steel boiler within its collapsing walls.

Nearby was an abandoned mine shaft, now frozen in, from the mouth of which an old handmade ladder protruded. In the other direction was another similar shaft. This one had a small homemade pipe boiler beside it and various pieces of mining paraphernalia scattered about. On the pile of tailings surrounding the shaft lay sections of riffles and fluming.

I made a simple sketch map of the location of these features and once I had compiled a description of the site for the Heritage Branch of the Yukon government, I speculated about what went on here.

Based on all my findings I concluded that late in the 1940s two men had spent the winter there, hand mining in the fashion employed in the early days of the gold rush. Checking the mining records, I discovered that a man named James Lanoff had purchased Claim Number 24 from another man in the 1930s, but I could find little about James Lanoff in the archives or any other written source.

This all changed, however, when in a conversation with long-time Yukon resident Earl Bennett I learned that he knew James (Jimmy) Lanoff and, what's more, they both worked for the Yukon Consolidate Gold Corporation, the company that dredged in the goldfields for decades. To my astonishment Earl told me that as a young man he had spent the winter of 1952 mining with Jimmy on this very claim. Over the next few years we had several conversations about that winter and what went on at Number 24.

I learned that the little homemade boiler produced enough steam to thaw the permanently frozen gravels that lay above bedrock when the men directed it through a hose to the bottom of the mine shaft. There, over a period of several winter months and labouring in poorly lit and cramped conditions twelve metres below the surface, Earl filled wooden buckets with the thawed paydirt, while up top Jimmy hauled them to the surface with a hand windlass greased with a slab of bacon. They maintained this structured routine in which each day they extracted a hundred buckets of thawed material and piled it up on the surface. Ten thousand buckets were dumped in anticipation of a spring cleanup.

Ironically, spring came and they had to go back to work for the dredge company—and they never got to recover the gold from the gravels they had laboured for months to dig up. When I stood on that tailing pile photographing the abandoned remains of their mine three decades later, I was actually on that pay gravel. Never has the passage from Robert Service seemed so appropriate: "... it isn't the gold that I'm wanting / So much as just finding the gold ..."

Gold Run proved to be one of the richest creeks in the fields, and I speculated about how much gold was hidden in that mound of gravel. We'll never know now, because in 1988 Teck Corporation, the company mining the block of claims on which this amazing treasure was found, bulldozed everything on the surface aside in preparation for mining the ground below. In fairness, the 10,000 buckets of pay were insignificant to a mining operation of this scale. The material the two men had laboured so hard all winter to recover would have been processed in a few hours by their modern screening plant.

Since 1982, I have visited Gold Run Creek many times, documenting the remains scattered about, as well as recording the progress of the new era of mining as Teck systematically worked up the valley. Never have I found another site that intrigued me as much as Claim Number 24. All that remains now is a record of what was there before this slice of history succumbed to the bulldozer's blade.

Later I learned more about Jimmy Lanoff, though the story is not yet complete. Jimmy was probably of Russian extraction. He mined in the Klondike region for decades. He was winchman on Dredge Number 9 on Sulphur Creek. When the dredging stopped because of the cold, Jimmy would head into Dawson where he loved to gamble at the Royal Alexandra Hotel. After Christmas he would go out to his claim on Gold Run to mine with his partner. In 1952, his partner went Outside for the winter, and young Earl was recruited for the job. Bill Diment, formerly from Dawson City and now retired and living at Marsh Lake, added another chapter to this story. Jimmy almost married Bill's mother, he told me, but backed out because of the age difference (nobody ever learned how old Jimmy really was). Nevertheless, Jimmy and Bill's mom remained good friends for many years, and Jimmy even supported the Diment family when Bill's father, Dick, went Outside to receive treatment for tuberculosis.

So a chance encounter with an abandoned mining claim on an obscure creek in the Klondike evoked strong images for me. And the story of this site and the men who lived and worked there is more touching, more genuine than anything one could ever dream up.

Fond Memories of Life at Bear Creek

It's been more than forty years since the company that was once the Yukon's largest employer shut down in 1966...

As we sat in their top-floor apartment overlooking downtown Whitehorse, Basil and Daphne Charman reminisced about life at Bear Creek.

"We brought the things to Whitehorse that we should have left behind," said Basil. "And we left behind the things we should have brought." But their vivid memories of life in Bear Creek, the community that housed the staff of the Yukon Consolidated Gold Corporation (also known as the YCGC), are mostly positive.

Bear Creek is located nine kilometres from Dawson City in the Klondike River valley, nestled into the dredge tailings near the mouth of the tributary of the same name. Daphne tells me that it was a great place to live and raise a family.

The men worked Monday through Friday and half days on Saturday while the women stayed home and took care of the kids. The hours on the job were long and the work very structured. Most families did not have an automobile, so the trip into Dawson City was an exceptional event. In those days before computers, there was only a local telephone network and radio station. There was no social-welfare net to catch you if you fell.

Basil first came to work for the YCGC in April of 1948, and his new bride, Daphne, whom he had married in October, followed him a month later. Their first home, perched on a low bench skirting the south side of the industrial complex that had grown up at the mouth of Bear Creek, had outdoor plumbing and no running water. The building cost them $400 and was about four metres square. Later they purchased a second cabin that they attached to the back of the first as a bedroom.

John Braga is repairing the impeller from a large pump in the big machine shop at Bear Creek. BASIL AND DAPHNE CHARMAN COLLECTION

At first, Basil received the labourer's wage of one dollar per hour and the work was seasonal—from April through November. He cut firewood and did odd jobs in the winter, and businesses in Dawson carried the seasonal employees on credit until they started work again in the spring. Basil spent

The inside of the machine shop at Bear Creek. BASIL AND DAPHNE CHARMAN COLLECTION

one year working at Granville about eighty kilometres away and another in the supply warehouse at Bear Creek.

Life got better when he began working year-round in the gigantic machine shop that was the centrepiece of the Bear Creek operation. Bud Rogers, shop foreman, and Teddy Ashton taught him to be a machinist, and he learned many of the other skills required to keep the company running smoothly.

Once Basil became a fulltime employee, the couple moved into housing on what was known as "The Island," an area of undredged ground on the opposite bank of the Klondike River, which once ran beside Bear Creek before the dredges moved the river channel to the far side of the valley.

The electricity provided by the company cost two dollars and fifty cents a month and was reliable except in the fall when the slush ice in the water supply interfered with the generation of current by the big turbines. Their house had a small 30-amp service, which meant that if they were heating food on the electric hot plate they had to be careful not to run any water, as the pump would place too much of a strain on the system and blow the fuse.

But Daphne, who was raised on a farm, didn't mind. When they lived in their first Bear Creek cabin, Basil would bring home five-gallon pails of water, carried with a shoulder yoke, from a tap in the machine shop. Once they moved onto The Island, they were supplied with cold running water. Telephone cost one dollar and twenty-five cents per month and operated on a party-line system. Each household had its own sequence of rings so that when the phone rang you would know who was to answer the call.

There were as many as a dozen men working in the machine shop, which operated year-round to repair faulty equipment and parts in preparation for the busy summer. Basil spent 90 percent of his time working on the lathe. When one of the welders repaired a broken shaft, it would next come to him to trim excess material off the surface and smooth it precisely to the desired dimension.

Even today the abandoned machine shop at Bear Creek is an impressive site. Large and high-ceilinged, it is still filled with countless tools from its working days. In one corner, row upon row of blacksmithing tools hang on wall racks, surrounding a large forge and gigantic mechanical hammer once used to shape red-hot steel into useful machinery parts.

Farther inside is where welders worked, opposite the babbit metal area where special molten alloys were poured into bearings to reduce friction. A small tool room is filled with cupboards and shelves lined with chisels and drill bits, each with a specific function. I can visualize Basil retrieving the tools he needed for his work from this room. In the centre of the building stands the pit that once housed the nine-hundred-ton press that would slip massive shafts into place on the large digging-ladder tumblers. Before this machine was installed workers sweated these parts together using the big crane outside the machine shop.

At the far end of the building were the drill presses and the lathes that were the tools of Basil's trade—tools that he came to know intimately during his many years with the company. The largest of these lathes was five metres long and dwarfed the men who worked at it.

By sharing personal knowledge and memories from their years of work for YCGC, people like Basil and Daphne Charman are helping to make these buildings and the inanimate objects they contain come alive for following generations. And we thank them for that.

The Secret Language of Gold

It didn't take me long to learn that placer mining has its own vocabulary. John Gould, my mentor in the study of gold mining, introduced me to this unique world when he took me out into the Klondike fields shortly after I arrived at my new job in Dawson City in 1978...

John Gould drove me around the Granville Loop, a circular route that follows up Hunker Creek and then descends Dominion Creek into the Indian River valley on the far side of the divide below King Solomon Dome. Granville is the most distant point on this route a hundred kilometres south of Dawson. From there, you can drive even farther south until you find yourself on the tributaries of the Stewart River, or you can continue along the loop that ascends Sulphur Creek until you reach the base of King Solomon Dome. At this point, you drive up a short, wretched road, best traversed in a four-wheel drive with plenty of clearance, to a viewpoint that looks out in all directions. From this height, the creeks radiate out like the spokes on a wheel—and every last one of them contains gold. From King Solomon Dome you can follow the road along a rocky ridge that divides the creeks into north flowing and south flowing. Eventually you will reach the summit above Bonanza Creek. Driving down that storied tributary you will pass through some of the most historic ground in the Klondike.

John introduced me to a human landscape with the marks of history cut

Box tenders are removing the riffles from the bottom of the sluice box so that they can collect the gold. This is known as a "cleanup." MICHAEL GATES

A sluicing operation on a mining claim in the 1980s: The backhoe at the top is feeding paydirt into the hopper where it is mixed with water. The gold is captured in the riffles, and the bulldozer in the foreground is moving the tailings out of the way. MICHAEL GATES

into its surface everywhere. Along this route he also taught me a vocabulary that has meaning to the people who mine gold for a living.

First, there are the place names. Many have been lifted from other famous goldfields: Black Hills Creek (South Dakota), Ballarat Creek (Australia) and Cripple Hill (Colorado). Others come from classical literature and ancient civilizations, such as Ophir (creek), derived from a Hebrew word for a spot noted in the Bible for its wealth. There are names derived from the Spanish tradition of gold seeking in Mexico and South America (El Dorado, Oro Grande and Oro Fino), as well as references to Greek (Eureka).

Reflecting the optimism of early prospectors, creeks were given hopeful names such as Gold Bottom, Gold Run, Big Gold, Little Gold, All Gold and Too Much Gold, while hills were labelled Nugget and Gold Hills.

Other places enshrined the history and traditions of the Klondike, as in creeks named after discoverers of gold: Carmack Fork (George Carmack), Henderson Creek (Robert Henderson), Skookum Gulch (Skookum Jim) and Hunker Creek (Andrew Hunker).

Placer miners have their own form of creation story that can be pinned to a specific location: Discovery. The discovery claim in any drainage system is the point from which all other claims are measured. Since the universal geographical unit of placer miners is the mining claim, all points and places can be measured in units equated with them. The Discovery Claim on Bonanza Creek is now enshrined by the Canadian government as a national historic site. Thus, Bonanza Creek, like many others, is divided into claims numbered up and down the stream in relation to Discovery Claim. When you visit Bonanza Creek during your summer vacation you might pan for gold on Claim 33, which is actually 33 Below Discovery (33B/D) on Bonanza Creek.

The small tributaries of the main creeks, called "pups," are also numbered in relation to Discovery. You might see "2 Below Pup," or "23 Gulch" on a map of the Klondike and like a sage tell the less informed that the number indicates how far that stream was from the discovery claim on that creek.

If there are many names to colourfully describe the places that dot the hills and valleys of the Klondike, there is even more language used to portray the actual act of gold extraction. To not know this vocabulary is to display your ignorance of placer mining. Miners talk about (cubic) yards of gravel moved. Historically, they measured the supply of water available for mining in "miner's inches." The sterile overlying deposits, which consist of "muck" and gravel, have to be stripped off to get down to the rich "pay streak" that generally lies on "bedrock." The amount of "overburden" removed is measured in cubic yards, as is the smaller volume of "paydirt" that is actually shovelled into the "sluice box."

This "paydirt" is flushed with large volumes of water over "riffles" that are used to trap the dense particles of gold (flakes, dust and nuggets) that are scattered widely (and hopefully in abundance) in the gravel. Miners measure their gold in the Troy Ounce, not the ounce that most of us are accustomed to, and when the miners have a "cleanup," they all hope that there are many ounces of gold left behind. A cleanup, incidentally, is the process of running a stockpile or "dump" of paydirt through a sluice plant to extract the gold.

In the early days of the gold rush the miners sank shafts and "drifted" (tunnelled horizontally along bedrock) by "burning" or thawing the frozen gravel. They often used "points," long steel tubes through which steam could be injected into the permafrost to melt the material so it could be excavated. Dredging, too, had its own language with "thawing" and "stripping" being performed before the boat (dredge) could excavate and process the gold-rich gravels of the valleys. They had special tools such as "point drivers" and "point jacks," and specialists or "point doctors" who knew how to keep the water flowing through the points. There were also particular jobs related to dredging, like "bow deckers," "stern deckers," "oilers" and "winchmen."

Many mining terms have come into general use in the English language. "Strike it rich" refers to finding a windfall at which point you would "stake your claim." Today, if things don't "pan out," or you find only "skim diggings," you can always go back to your old job stocking shelves at the supermarket.

The voice of the Klondike goldfields is rich with lore and tradition. If you want to stake your claim on the 135-year history of placer mining, you will have to learn the language too. Otherwise, your expectations may simply not pan out.

Coming of Age in the Goldfields

While many people of the Yukon have long maligned famed-author Pierre Berton, calling him arrogant, I had an opportunity to see another side of the man. I once accompanied him into the Territorial Administration Building where he pointed out the old wheeled cart that his father, a mining recorder, used to roll into the vault at the end of the workday with a young Pierre hanging on as passenger. We talked about books during his visits and when I wrote my own (Gold at Fortymile Creek) he encouraged me. In the 1980s, immersed in historical work on the goldfields, I asked him if he would be willing to share his experiences and he immediately agreed, always generous with his time.

The restaurant at the Midnight Sun Hotel was noisy with the clatter of dishes and clamour of voices as we settled in our booth. It was Discovery Day, 1985. Pierre Berton had arranged for an hour outside of his busy Dawson schedule to talk to me about coming of age and working for "The Company" during the summers of 1937, '38 and '39.

"The Company" was the massive dredging operation known as the Yukon Consolidated Gold Corporation, but "The Company" was all you had to say because everyone knew what it was.

The Company facilitated Berton's emergence into manhood as it did for many young men. By the time I caught up with them in the early 1980s, these men had reached the end of their careers and could reflect on this rite of passage.

It was the Great Depression and jobs were hard to come by. Berton's father, Frank, had been superannuated by the government from his position as mining recorder in Dawson City. They lived in Victoria on his tiny pension while Pierre and his sister, Lucy, went to school.

When Frank was offered his old job back, an offer no one could refuse in those hard times, he left the family and returned alone to Dawson City. Through his connections with the executives of The Company (Frank Berton was good friends with W.H.S. McFarland, the general manager) he was able to get his teenage son a job working on a thawing crew on Middle Dominion Creek some eighty kilometres from Dawson.

Berton was so green that when he was hired in July 1937 and sent from Bear Creek to Dominion Creek in the back of a rattling old truck, as a prank they hung a tag around his neck that said "Middle Dominion Camp." He naively thought this was normal procedure, which it certainly was not, as he was laughingly reminded by one of the other fellows on the thawing crew decades later during a return visit to Dawson.

The work was hard and unrelenting. Day after day he went out to the

A network of pipes and points in a thawing operation in the Klondike goldfields. YUKON ARCHIVES, COUTTS COLLECTION 83/94, PHOTO #70

One man uses a point twister, while the other, standing on the ladder, hammers the thawing point into the frozen earth. Steam is forced into the ground through the hollow steel "point," where it thaws the ground in preparation for mining. YUKON ARCHIVES, JOHN WELLS COLLECTION 84/80, PHOTO #18

flats on Dominion Creek to set up pipe and keep the water flowing through the intricate network of pipes and hoses to the hollow steel tubes, or thawing points, that they drove into the frozen ground. Two decades before, they had determined that cold water was more cost-effective than steam for thawing the frozen ground.

Berton quickly learned not to mention his university studies. Out in the goldfields nobody cared. Nor could he see any point to this work where, he reflected, they took the gold out of the ground only to ship it to Fort Knox to put it back into the ground. It was just a paycheque for the young Berton.

Nevertheless, over those three summers he became a man. He learned to work, he learned to drink, and he learned the ways of the world. On June 21, 1939—the longest day of the year—a truck rolled into camp just as the men were retiring to the bunkhouse for the evening. Someone shouted, "Anyone for Fournier's?" and into the truck and off they went to Joe Fournier's roadhouse at the top of the divide between Hunker and Dominion creeks.

Someone offered Berton a drink of whiskey in a tone that brooked no refusal. By the time he reached the roadhouse he was already halfway to roaring drunk. From Fournier's, someone suggested they drive down Hunker Creek road to Gold Bottom where there was another roadhouse with a dance going on. They stole Fournier's truck and off they went.

On the return trip they ran off the road, overturning the truck. Berton alternately walked, staggered and ran down the road back to camp. Through good fortune, a truck came by, picked him up and deposited him, still drunk, at the mess hall with ten minutes to spare before his workday commenced. He didn't know that Joe Fournier was going to throw the book at him for his antics.

For many of the others I spoke to about their experiences working for The Company, the memories were equally indelible. Matt Offer got a job as a flunky and then as bull cook in one of the mess halls. Later he advanced to bow decker on one of the dredges. With a tear in his eye as he talked, he remembered that this was his first real job.

Another was John Calam, a retired university professor, who in the summer of 1999 travelled with me to the site of the dredge camp at Granville where he had laboured a half century before. He had an almost photographic recall of working on the thawing and stripping crew there. We stood beside the road at the site on Dominion Creek where the row of bunkhouses used to be, now merely grass and bush and a few pits in the gravel. I watched transfixed as John pulled a harmonica out of his pocket and played a mournful tune as he had once done as a young man on the porch of the bunkhouse. His eyes teared up as he played, and it took him a moment before he could speak again. I think he had been waiting a long time to play that tune once more at Granville.

Another man who made a return visit was Ted Thornton Trump, who worked at the company headquarters at Bear Creek though he also went out into the goldfields. Ted went on to become an inventor, most notably of the hydraulic cherry-picker, which is used today by linemen working on electrical transformers.

Trump came back to Dawson to repay an act of kindness. Decades before, the Gould family had allowed him to stay in their house in Dawson until he was able to hire on with The Company. Now a wealthy man he flew my wife and me and John and Madeleine Gould to Inuvik for lunch before taking us out over the Beaufort Sea and returning to Dawson. For each of these men there was something special in their experience of working for The Company. Something that made them return one last time.

And Pierre Berton's wild ride? Both John Gould and biographer A.B. McKillop comment on this episode. Fournier laid charges against Berton for stealing the truck—and Berton thought for sure that he was going to jail. His father told him to get back to Vancouver as fast as possible, and then hired Charlie McLeod, The Company's lawyer, to handle the predicament. According to John, when the case came before Judge McCauley the judge looked at Fournier, for whom he had no love, and then looked at the charges and announced: "Case dismissed."

I think Frank Berton may have called in a favour or two. And it's a good thing. Imagine one of Canada's foremost authors with a criminal record!

The Yukon River Breakup Brings
a Flood of Excitement

May marks the time of the breakup of ice on the Yukon River. This event is one of prime importance in Dawson City, and everything in town comes to an abrupt halt when the frozen river unlocks. In the days preceding the breakup, everybody walks along the waterfront dike eyeing the fragmenting ice and speculating with others about when it will move. Along with the conjecture is the anxiety and concern about whether or not the Yukon will overflow its bank—and hence wreak havoc throughout the town.

The ice broke on the Yukon River at Dawson City at 12:17 p.m. on Sunday, May 3, 2009. It was a quiet affair. Such is not always the case. This same year, misfortune struck Eagle, Alaska, which experienced the worst flooding in living memory. The Yukon River rose to record levels and numerous homes and businesses were smashed to bits by massive blocks of river ice.

All spring, Yukoners had been buying their IODE (Imperial Order of the Daughers of the Empire) Dawson ice pool tickets, everyone hopeful that they had chosen the winning time. That's the moment that the ice in front of town starts to move, and the clock, attached to the tripod on the offshore ice, stops. The lucky ticket holder wins the prize money as well as the bragging rights for guessing correctly.

Ice is pushing down the Fortymile River (foreground) into the Yukon (centre), where the town of Forty Mile is threatened by the rising waters, ca. 1896. YUKON ARCHIVES, D'ARCY EDWARD STRICKLAND FONDS, PHOTO # 09400

Breakup is just one of the many special annual happenings that dot the Dawson calendar. In the old days when the siren went off, announcing that the ice was moving, everyone flocked to the waterfront to watch. Clerks would abandon their cash registers, students their seats and parishioners their pews to witness this important annual event. Immediately after, people would start eyeing the river uneasily, apprehensive about whether the ice would jam and the water rise.

I was new to Dawson City in 1979 when breakup occurred. We had endured a particularly cold winter, with thick river ice and plenty of snow. April brought with it unseasonably warm weather. The combination had catastrophic results for the Klondike capital.

As May began, the community started taking defensive measures to prepare for the possibility of high water. Crews were out sandbagging along Front Street and the entire community pitched in. I was house-sitting for my future wife while she was on holiday in England. On the evening of May 2, I retreated to her tiny trailer where I listened to the emergency announcements on CBC Radio and waited. Sometime after midnight, on the morning of May 3, the generator providing electricity for the community shut down and the town was eerily silent.

In the twilight that befalls Dawson at that time of year I could see strange shadows and a liquid darkness that crept up the hill toward me. As the light returned I witnessed the extent of the damage that had befallen my new community.

From a neighbouring house Alan Nordling, a refugee from the dark rushing waters, joined me. We seconded a nearby canoe beached on the new shoreline halfway up the hillside and paddled through Dawson to witness the devastation. I looked across the vast expanse of water that now filled the entire bottom of the Yukon valley. A rapidly moving current carried large blocks of ice that surged through the community. At the corner of King Street and Third Avenue, we paused to take a breather. Only by clinging to the stop sign on the corner of the intersection could I prevent us from being washed away by the flow of freezing water.

The flooding was the worst in the short history of the community. It cost millions of dollars to repair the damage, and took years to fully recover.

Looking down Queen Street toward the Yukon River, May 3, 1979.
MICHAEL GATES

Hopefully, the dike constructed in 1986 along the waterfront will protect Dawson from future catastrophes.

I quickly learned that this was not the first time flooding had occurred in a Yukon town. In fact, riverside communities such as Old Crow, Mayo, Ross River and even Whitehorse have had their own encounters with high water. The first well-documented flood took place in 1896. By the beginning of that May, all eyes in the tiny community of Forty Mile, at the mouth of the Fortymile River, looked toward the Yukon River in anticipation. Being gamblers at heart, the men of Forty Mile started numerous pools, betting on the day, hour and minute the ice would unlock. People stayed up late scrutinizing the river, and a night watchman was appointed to rouse any sleeping citizens when it broke, as this is when the danger of flooding is greatest.

Breakup was later than usual and the wait became so monotonous that the watchman actually sounded the alarm falsely just to satisfy his need of company. Everyone then retired again and he continued his vigil. On the fourteenth, the Fortymile River finally broke up and flushed its ice onto the ice still locked in place on the Yukon River. Then, on the seventeenth, the cry went up: the Yukon River was moving! Huge blocks of ice ground together and gyrated crazily.

The ice jammed a few kilometres below Forty Mile and the water level rose more than five metres in an hour and a half, reaching the sugar bins in the Alaska Commercial Company store. Everyone prepared to evacuate town. The bridge crossing the slough behind the main cluster of buildings washed away. One man, thinking that the end had come, jumped into his boat and paddled up the Fortymile River. Another was forced to climb up onto the roof of his cabin where he completed the shave that had been interrupted by the sudden rise of water. The Anglican mission, located on an island, was particularly vulnerable. When the water rushed in, Bishop Bompas and other members of the mission party were forced up into the loft.

While the jam broke a couple of days later, the water ran high for several more before receding and leaving a line of icebergs, uprooted trees and debris in its wake. Life then returned to normal very quickly in Forty Mile, and on May 25 the North-West Mounted Police led a celebration of the Queen's birthday with a volley of gunfire.

Dawson City was hit by a flood during the height of the gold rush in the spring of 1898. Before the big deluge of 1979 the other most noteworthy inundations occurred in 1925 and 1944. In the 1960s there were two more. The *Dawson Daily News* declared the flood in 1925 to have been the worst ever. It made the same claim in May of 1944.

On May 4, 1944, the water of the Yukon rose nearly three metres. The ice moved the following day at 1:27 p.m., making Charley Mason of Moosehide richer by more than $8,000. When the waters finally reached town the torrent flowed down Fifth Avenue. Minto Park, just south of the Territorial Administration Building, turned into a lake, and the force of the ice flowing in the main channel did serious damage to the pilings supporting the wharf on the waterfront. Being wartime, the military was called upon to assist. A "Flying Fortress" B-19 was flown in to drop a load of bombs on the ice jam. This had no effect. Dawson recovered, of course, living on to suffer through more floods.

Mother Nature has a mind of her own. We may prepare with sandbags and evacuation plans but when the waters rise, there is not much we can do but watch and wait.

Index

Aishihik, village of, 38, 133
Alaska Daily Empire, 182
Alsek River, 18, 24, 44–47, 132
Amos, Bridget and Dorian, 192
Ashton, Teddy, 237
Association of Business Men (ABM), 199–200

Baker, Terry, 72–73
Banks, Della Murray, 124–**126**–**127**–**128**–129, 140
Bass, Fred, 228
Bear Creek, village of, 227, 234–38, 248
Beebe, Bera, **167**, 168–69
Beebe, Iola, **167**, 168–69
Belaney, Archibald Stansfeld (Grey Owl), 180
Benedek, Kristin, 49
Bennett, Earl, 232
Bennett, Jim, 11, 18
Bennett, Richard Bedford, 158
Bennett, town of, **86**–87
Bennett Lake, 74
Berry, Bill, 55–**57**
Berry, Clarence, 56–57, 107
Berton, Frank, 245, 248
Berton, Laura, 189, 215
Berton, Lucy, 245
Berton, Pierre, 145, 215, 244–45, 247–48
Black, George, 94–97, 158–61, **189**–191
Black, Martha (née Munger), 94–97, 158–**159**–161
Blanchard, Paul, 97
Bleeker, Henry, 103
Bompas, William, 61, 69, 252
Bonanza Creek, 73, 145, 165, 242
Bond, Jeff, 44–47
Bonnifield, Sam, 110
Borden, Robert, 206
Boss, Annie, 33
Boss, Jim (Kashxóot), 31–**32**–34
Boyle, Adelina (Kitty), 168–69
Boyle, Joseph Whiteside (Klondike Joe), 123, 145–**146**–148, **167**

Bratnober, Henry, 77
Brewster, Art, 18–20
Brewster, Dale, 18
British Empire Club, 199
Brown, Charles, 61–63, 195
Burley, David, 225
Burns, Pat, 136

Campbell, Robert, 26–28
Carmack, George Washington, 73, 164, 242
Carmacks, town of (Carmack's Post), 29, 115, 122
Cassidy, Steve, 85
Castillo, Victoria, 91–**92**–93
Champagne, village of, 18, 115
Charman, Basil and Daphne, 234–38
Chrétien, Jean, 98
Chilkat Pass, 28–29, 38, 77, 115, 123, 139–40
Chilkoot Pass, 60, 202
Chilkoot Trail, 85–**86**–**87**–**88**–89
Circle City, Alaska, 63, 73, 121, 164, 211
Clayson, Fred, 99–102
Clayson, Will, 100
Clements, Gus, 69
Commissioner's Residence, 94–**95**–**96**–98
Congdon, Frederick T., 96, 187, 190, 206–07
Constantine, Charles, 61, 63, 64–65, 68, 69, 72–73, **163**–64, 195

Daily Klondike Nugget, **101**, 176–**177**–179
Dalton, Jack, 18, 24, 38, 76–77, 115–**117**–119, 121, 136, 137, 139
Dalton Post, 18, 35, 115
Dalton Trail, 115–16, 118, 134–**135**–136, 138–**140**
Davidson, George, 27, 29
Dawson Amateur Athletic Association (DAAA), 225, 227
Dawson Charley, 164

Dawson City, 71, 109–**111**–112, **122**, 147, 175
  alcohol in, 62, 69–70, 197–**198**–200
  architecture, 94–**95**–**96**–98, **150**, 153, **172**–**173**, 195, 205–**207**–208
  cattle drive to, 118, 134–**135**–137, 139
  crime, 103, 210–12
  food shortage of 1897, 120–**122**–123, 130–**131**–133
  prostitution, 213–**214**–**215**–**216**–217
Dawson Daily News, 182, **188**, 190, 199, 226, 253
Dawson Film Find, 225–28
De Laguna, Frederica, 44
Delgrande, Luigi, 97
Densmore, Frank, 195
Diment, Bill, 233
Dominion Creek, 176, 239, 245, 247–48
Dowdell, Grant, 98
drift mining, 58, 105
Dry Bay, Alaska, 37, 44, 46, 47
Duncan, Paddy, 156
Dunn, Pete, 91
"Dutch" Kate, 213
Dyea, Alaska, 78, 80

Eagle, Alaska, 211, 249
Easton, Norm, 39–**40**–**41**–43
Ellis, Emma, 44

Fawcett, Thomas, 176
Fort Constantine, 64–**65**–**66**–**67**–68
Fort Cudahy, 61, 63, 65
Fort Reliance, 162
Fort Selkirk, 26–**28**–30, 76, 115, 121
Fortin, Emilie. *See* Tremblay, Emilie (née Fortin)
Fortin, Joseph, 88
Fortymile River, 55–**56**–**57**–59, 64, 69, 78, 163, 193, **250**, 252
Forty Mile townsite, 55, 60–**62**–63, 64, 71, 134, 163–64, 171–72, **193**–195, 213, **250**, 252

Fournier, Joe, 247–48
Franklin, Howard, 78
Franklin, John, 75
Franklin, R.E., 212
Fraser, Johnny, 18
French Joe, 71
Fuller, Thomas W., 96

Gates, Kathy, 11, 180, 229,
    230–31
Gates, William C. (Bill
    Swiftwater), 123,
    166–**167**–169
Gendreau, Pierre, 205
Girouard, Mr. (Registrar),
    187–88
Glacier Creek, 72–73
Glave, Edward J., 18–**19**, 24,
    76–77, 118
Gold Bottom Creek, 164,
    242
Gold Run Creek, 230–**231**–
    233, 242
Gould, John, 55, 239, 248
Gould, Madeleine, 248
Grand Forks, 188, 214
Grant, Leroy, 153
Granville, 215, 230, 239,
    247–48
Graves (murderer), 99–100,
    102
Greer, Sheila, 51
Grey Owl (Archibald
    Stansfeld Belaney), 180

Haines, Alaska (Haines
    Mission), 115–17, 123,
    132, 157
Haines Junction, 46–47
Hamilton, C.H., 61, 62, 71
Hanlon, Bill, 50
Hansen, Captain J.E., 120
Hare, Greg, 50
Hartmier, Richard, 231
Hawthorn, Mont, 116
Hayes, C. Willard, 75–76
Hayne, Sergeant M.H.E.,
    66, 69
Hedgecock, Christine, 88,
    89, 222
Henderson, Robert, 164, 242
Henry, Billy, 136–37
Hik, David, 48–49
Historic Sites and
    Monuments Board of
    Canada, 33, 97, 145, 147,
    161, 174, 216

Hornsby, J.A., 181
Hunker, Andrew, 242
Hunker Creek, 239, 242
Hutchi (Hootchy-Eye), vil-
    lage of, 32, 38, 122, 132

Imperial Order of the
    Daughters of the Empire
    (IODE), 161, 249
Innes-Taylor, Alan, 35

Jackson, Sheldon, 131–32
Jackson, T.W., 31–32
John, Bessie, 42
Johnny, Eldred, 42
Johnny, Tommy, 42
Johnson, Ben, 97
Johnson, Linda, 29
Johnson, Simon, 89
Jones, Ed and Star, 88
Jones, Kathy, 227, 229
Jones, Tom, 59
Judge, William Henry, 112,
    170–**171**–**172**–174
Juneau, Alaska, 76, 117, 118,
    182

Kent, William S., 89
King, William Lyon
    Mackenzie, 207
King Solomon Dome, 214,
    239
Klondike City (Lousetown),
    215
Klondike Korner, 227
Klukwan, Alaska, 28–29,
    36–37
Kohklux (Chilkat Tlingit
    chief), 29–30
Kohklux map, 26–**27**–30
Kula, Sam, **226**–228
Kusawa Lake, 29, 49
Kuzyk, Gerry, 49
Kwädąy Dän Ts'ìnchį, 24, 51

Ladue, Joe, 71, 164
Lake Laberge, 31–33, 137
Lamore, Belle (Nellie the
    Pig), 168
Lamore, Grace, 168
Lamore, Gussie, 167–69
Lande (Jim Boss's mother),
    32
Lanoff, James (Jimmy), 232,
    233
Lesniak, Peter, 217

Licensed Victuallers'
    Association (LVA), 199
Lindeman Lake, 86, 88, 89
Little John site, 39–**41**–43
London, Jack, 138, 198
Lousetown (Klondike City),
    215
Lovejoy, Diamond Tooth
    Gertie, 178
Lowell Glacier, 44–47

MacBride Museum of Yukon
    History, 33, 44, 46, 77
MacLean, Constance,
    149–53
Madison, Henry, 78
Maguire, Philip Ralph, 102
Mandy, Madge, 157
Mann, Charles C., 23
Mason, Charley, 253
Mason, Skookum Jim
    (Keish), 164
Mathes, J.W., 88
McCauley, C.A., 248
McClellan, Catharine, 24–25
McCook, James C., **176**–179
McCue, James, 88
McFarland, W.H.S., 245
McGee, Thomas, 121–23
McGinnis, Dan (Jack),
    115–19
McKay, Dave, 165
McKay, Glen, 42
McKeown, Martha, 116
McLeod, Charlie, 248
McPhee, William (Bill), 57,
    164, 195
McQuesten Post, 189
McQuesten, Jack, 62–63, 78,
    162, 195
Mercer, Sadelle, 169
Miles Canyon, 74, 80
Miller Creek, 201–04
miners' committee, 61,
    71–73, 162–65
Minto, 99
Mitchell, Alaska. *See* Forty
    Mile townsite
Montreal Marie, 187
Mount St. Elias. *See* St. Elias
    Mountains
Mounties. *See* North-West
    Mounted Police
Muncaster, Arabelle
    Frances (née Patchen),
    154–**155**–157
Muncaster, Bill, 156–57

Mundessa (Jim Boss's father), 32
Munger, George Merrick, Jr., 159
Munger, Martha. *See* Black, Martha (née Munger)
Munns, Judy, 180

Neskatahéen, village of, 18, 24, 35–37–38, 115
Neumiller, Betty, 215–16
Newman, Margie, 110
Nielson, Jacob, 212
Nome Nugget, 182
Noogaayík, village of, 17
Nordling, Alan, 251
North-West Mounted Police, 60–63, 69–70–72–73, 87, 121, 130–31, 195, 210–12
  at Fort Constantine, 64–68
  as mining recorder, 163–164
  and the O'Brien murders, 99–103
  at Tagish Post, 90–91–92–93
Noyes, Thomas, 155–56

O'Brien, George, 99–101–103
O'Brien, Thomas, 135
O'Brien, T.W., 62, 195
Oatley Sisters, 110
Offer, Matt, 247
Ogilvie, William, 31, 60, 71, 165, 194, 205, 210
Olsen, Lawrence, 99–101–102
Order of the Midnight Sun, 211

Palace Grand Theatre, 228
Paradise Alley, 178, 213, 217
Patchen, Arabelle Frances. *See* Muncaster, Arabelle Frances (née Patchen)
Pattullo, Thomas Dufferin, 206–08
Pearson, Constable E.E., 87
Pennycuick, Alexander, 102
People's Prohibition Movement (PPM), 199

Portus B. Weare, 63, 64
Powell, John Wesley, 75–76
Primrose, P.C.H., 210
Purdy, Martha. *See* Black, Martha (née Munger)
Purdy, Will Amon, 159

Queen Marie of Romania, 145, 148

Rabbit Creek, 73, 164, 172
Rae, Lana, 230
Reeves, Brian, 97
Reid, Frank, 181
Relfe, Lynn, 99–103
Riggs, Thomas, 182–83
Rivard, Rene, 89
Roback, Frances, 18
Roch, Mike, 50–51
Rogers, Bud, 237
Russell, Mark, 76
Ryan, Patrick, 99

Schwatka, Frederick, 60, 74–75–77
Scott, Ruby, 216
Sears, Dann, 89
self-dumper, 107
Service, Robert, 130, 149–150–151–153, 233
Shakely, James, 210
Shank (Chilkat medicine man), 18
Shape, William, 141
Shäwshe. *See* Little John site. *See also* Neskatahéen *and* Dalton Post
Sidney, Rae-Ann, 91
Sifton, Clifford, 211
Silks, Mattie, 213–14
Singh, Patrick, 109
Sisters of St. Ann, 97, 171, 173, 205–06
Skagway News, 181
Smith, Austin, 91
Smith, Bill, 71
Smith, Elijah, 33
Smith, Jefferson (Soapy), 181
Snow, George T., 195
Spurr, Josiah, 195
Squam, Joe, 32
Squaw Creek, 156–57
St. Elias Mountains, 48, 75–76

Strickland, D'Arcy, 63, 64–65, 67, 72–73
Strong, Annie Hall, 181, 183
Strong, John Franklin Alexander, 180–181–183

Tagish Lake, 85, 90
Tagish Post, 90–91–92–93
Tatshenshini River, 17–21, 23–25, 35, 37, 38, 44, 50
Taylor, June, 58
Taylor, Larry, 55–57–59
Thompson, Alfred, 187, 207
Thomson, Clifford, 227
Thorp, Willis, 134, 139–40
Tremblay, Emilie (née Fortin), 88, 201–203–204
Tremblay, Pierre Nolasque (Jack), 202, 204
Troll, Gypsy, 215
Troy, John W., 182
Trudeau, Pierre Elliott, 32, 33
Trump, Ted Thornton, 248
Tweedsmuir Glacier, 46

Walker, D.W., 69
Walsh, James Morrow, 206
Ward, Warren, 50–51
West, Kid, 103
Whitcomb, J.F., 85
White Pass, 92, 137, 139, 147
White River First Nation, 42–43
White River, 76–77, 133
Whitehorse, 32–33, 92, 151, 197, 204, 211, 252
Wickersham, James, 182
Wild, Tom, 18
Williams, J.A., 69
Williams, Tom, 78–81
Woods, Patrick, 116–17

Yukon Consolidated Gold Corporation (YCGC), 195, 234–235–236–238, 244–48
Yukon News, 217

Zazula, Grant, 91
Zazula, Roman, 91